P9-CSA-711

LAW IN AMERICA

MODERN LIBRARY CHRONICLES

CHINUA ACHEBE on Africa
KAREN ARMSTRONG on Islam
DAVID BERLINSKI on mathematics
RICHARD BESSEL on Nazi Germany
IAN BURUMA on modern Japan
IAN BURUMA and AVISHAI MARGALIT on Occidentalism
JAMES DAVIDSON on the Golden Age of Athens
SEAMUS DEANE on the Irish
FELIPE FERNÁNDEZ-ARMESTO on the Americas
PAUL FUSSELL on World War II in Europe
MARTIN GILBERT on the Long War, 1914–1945
PETER GREEN on the Hellenistic Age
JAN T. GROSS on the fall of Communism
ALISTAIR HORNE on the age of Napoleon
PAUL JOHNSON on the Renaissance
TONY JUDT on the Cold War
FRANK KERMODE on the age of Shakespeare
JOEL KOTKIN on the city
HANS KÜNG on the Catholic Church
BERNARD LEWIS on the Holy Land
FREDRIK LOGEVALL on the Vietnam War
MARK MAZOWER on the Balkans
JOHN MICKLETHWAIT and ADRIAN WOOLDRIDGE
on the company
PANKAJ MISHRA on the rise of modern India
ANTHONY PAGDEN on peoples and empires
RICHARD PIPES on Communism
COLIN RENFREW on prehistory
JOHN RUSSELL on the museum
KEVIN STARR on California
ALEXANDER STILLE on fascist Italy
CATHARINE R. STIMPSON on the university
MICHAEL STÜRMER on the German Empire
STEVEN WEINBERG on science
BERNARD WILLIAMS on freedom
A. N. WILSON on London
ROBERT S. WISTRICH on the Holocaust
GORDON S. WOOD on the American Revolution
JAMES WOOD on the novel

LAWRENCE M. FRIEDMAN

LAW IN AMERICA

A Short History

A MODERN LIBRARY CHRONICLES BOOK

THE MODERN LIBRARY

NEW YORK

Library of Congress Cataloging-in-Publication Data

Friedman, Lawrence Meir.
Law in America : a short history/ Lawrence M. Friedman.—
Modern Library ed.
p. cm. — (A Modern Library chronicles book ; 10)
Includes bibliographical references and index.
ISBN 0-375-50635-7
1. Law—United States—History. I. Title.
II. Modern Library chronicles ; 10.
KF352 .F73 2002
349.73—dc21
2002071423

To Leah, Jane, Amy, Sarah, Paul, David, and Lucy

ACKNOWLEDGMENTS

Many people have helped me in my work over the years—students, colleagues, family—and their influence and support can be felt on every page, even if they did not literally contribute to the writing of this book. I do want to acknowledge the wonderful help I have always gotten, on this and every other project, from my assistant, Mary Tye, and from the Stanford Law Library, in particular Paul Lomio, Erika Wayne, and David Bridgman, three members of its marvelous staff.

CONTENTS

ONE

INTRODUCTION

At my university (Stanford) I teach a course to undergraduates called Introduction to American Law. On my way to class, on the first day—the class usually meets at nine o'clock, and it is a tough assignment to keep the students awake—I buy a copy of the *Chronicle,* the morning newspaper from San Francisco. When I begin the class, after the first few announcements and the like, I wave the paper in front of the class, and read some of the headlines. The point I want to get across to the students is that *every* domestic story in the front part of the newspaper, before you get to the recipes and the comics and the sports pages, has a legal angle—has some connection with the legal system. Of course, I have no control over the newspaper, but the trick never fails. Almost invariably, *every* story about public life in the United States, or private life interesting enough to get into the newspaper, will mention a law, a legal proposal, a bill in Congress or in the state legislature, or something a judge, a policeman, a court, a lawyer has done or said; or some statement from the president or other high officials, in any case always about some affair or situation or event done by, with, through, or against the law. In the world we live in—the country we live in—almost nothing has more impact on our lives, nothing is more entangled with our everyday existence, than that something we call the *law.* This is a startling fact; and it gets the students' attention—as it should.

Why is it the case that the newspapers are so full of material about the legal system? What makes law so central to American society? Where does all this law come from? Is all of this emphasis on law and legal matters good for the country, or is it a sign of some deep-seated pathology? What *is* American law, and how did it get this way? These questions are the subject of this short book. What I am trying to do is provide a historical introduction to American law—or, perhaps more accurate, to American legal culture; or, perhaps, to the spirit of American law, and how it has related, over time, to American society in general.

Before we go any further, I have to say a word or two about the *definition* of "law." There are, in fact, many ways to define this elusive term, and many ways to describe what we mean by "law." For now, I want to adopt a simple, but broad and workable definition. Law is, above all, collective action: action through and by a government. When I say "the law," I really mean "the legal system." The legal system includes, first of all, a body of rules—the "laws" themselves. Some of these are federal laws, enacted by Congress, some come from state legislatures, some are ordinances of city governments. Then there are literally tens of thousands of rules and regulations— from the Food and Drug Administration or the Securities and Exchange Commission or the Forest Service or the board that licenses doctors in Minnesota, or from local zoning boards or school boards or any of the dozens and dozens of agencies at every level of government. But all these, in themselves, are nothing but pieces of paper. What makes them come alive (when they do) are the people and the institutions that produce, interpret, and enforce them. This means police, jails, wardens, courts, judges, postal workers, FBI agents, the secretary of the treasury; it means civil servants who work for all the agencies in Washington, in the state capitals, and in city hall; and the inspectors who go out to factories and businesses, or who make sure that elevators are safe, or who put their stamp of approval on slabs of meat. It also means the lawyers (nearly a million of them) who advise people on how to follow the rules or cope with the rules or get around the rules, or how to use them to their best advantage. The lawyers are a vital part of the system, just as teachers are essential to the educational system, and doctors and nurses are essential to the medical system. And "the legal system" is the way all of these people and institutions interact with one another, and with the general public.

What I outlined is, I think, a useful way to look at the law or the legal system. There are other ways as well. I spoke generally in terms of something readers could identify as "government"; what the government did or does, and how people use or react to government—broadly defined that is, so that the policeman at a busy intersection, straightening out traffic, is part of the system, just as much as the chief justice of the United States is part of the system. There are even broader ways of defining law. It can be looked at as a kind of *process*, which does not have to be connected with a "government" at all. Universities, factories, hospitals, big companies—these also often have a kind of "legal system," quite internal, quite "private." Law can, in other words, be official or unofficial; governmental or private. It can also be *formal* or *informal*. A big trial is a very formal procedure. It is governed by a network of formal rules. When a policeman breaks up a fight and tells two drunks to go home, this is a "legal" action—an action by an official, whose power comes from law—but it is also fairly informal. It follows no strict rules, and leaves no paper trail behind. All societies, in a sense, have a "legal system." They all have rules and ways to enforce the rules. Big, complex societies have big, complex systems. *Within* big, complex societies are smaller subgroups, down to individual families; and even families have ways to make rules and enforce them (sometimes, if the children are teenagers, without much success). The "law" inside a family is usually not written down, and "procedures" are pretty informal.

But the big society needs formality; it cannot go on without formality—without rules, especially rules of law. This is because a big society is made up of millions of people, who interact with each other in complicated ways. Strangers meet and affect other strangers many times each day: on the street, in elevators, airplanes, stores, and workplaces. In many ways, our very lives are in the hands of strangers. Consider, for example, taking a plane from San Francisco to Chicago. A jet airplane is an awesome machine. It flies high above the clouds; and if something goes wrong, your life is at stake. What guarantee do you have that the plane was well put together? That the maintenance is up-to-date? How do we know that the pilot knows what he is doing? How can we be sure that the air controllers will do their job? We have no *personal* knowledge or control over any of these people—not the pilot, not the air controllers, not the maintenance crew, or the factory workers who worked on the plane. For this, and a hundred other daily events, people have to rely on something else. That something else is the law. There is a social demand for rules and regulations about air safety, the way planes are made, air traffic control, and so on. Of course, a society can function without such rules—people can take chances, if they wish. But in the modern state, the social demand for *regulation* is a fact; and air safety is one of the fields where the demand is quite strong. After the terrible tragedy at the World Trade Center on September 11, 2001, the demand for more rules— for more law, for tougher law—became especially marked.

In simple, face-to-face societies, custom, habits, and traditions do most of the heavy lifting as far as enforcing the norms is concerned. But in a complex society, a heterogeneous society, a society where the interactions between strangers are pervasive, a society where people buy food and clothes, instead of growing and making these themselves, a society made up of many different groups and many different ways of thinking, custom loses its bite, traditions give up their grip, and society comes to depend on other ways to control whatever forces and objects and people the society wants to control. This mechanism is what we call *law*. Social control still, of course, depends heavily on customs, habits, and traditions; and the law does not come out of nowhere—it builds on these customs, habits, and traditions; but it adds to them the bite and the sting of collective rules and collective enforcement.

This of course would be true of any modern society. It would be just as true of Italy or Japan as it is true of the United States. And, in fact, all of these societies (and their legal systems) do have a lot in common. But they also, all of them, have features that make them distinctive, unique. What is distinctive about *American* law—compared, say, to the law of Italy or Japan?

To begin with, our legal system is a common law system. The common law is one of many *families* of legal systems in the world. Legal systems come in clusters—clusters of relatives. Legal systems are a little bit like languages in this regard. French, Spanish, and Italian are Romance languages: they are independent languages, but they have a lot in common, mostly because they have a common ancestor, Latin. English, German, and Dutch also have a lot in common, because they also have a common ancestor (though it was never a written language). Most of the legal systems of Europe belong to a single great family, often called the *civil law* family. Many concepts and terms within the civil law family reflect the influence of Roman law, the remote ancestor of these systems. In the Middle Ages—to make a long story short—Roman law was rediscovered, reworked, and "received" by most European societies; it began to be studied in the universities, and it became the basis of the various national systems.[1]

There was one prominent European holdout: the English. They never took part in the "reception" of Roman law. Instead, they on the whole stayed true to their native system, the so-called common law. As things turned out, the English became lords of a huge empire; and they carried their language and their legal system with them throughout the empire. The common law therefore became the basis of the legal systems in all the English-speaking colonies (though not only in those). It was natural for settlers in, say, Massachusetts or Australia to make use of the only legal system they knew and were familiar with, just as it was only natural for them to use the only *language* they were familiar with, which was English. Just as the sun never set on the British empire at its height, it never set on the old common law.

The common law, then, forms the raw material of the law of England, its colonies, its former colonies, and the colonies of colonies. It is the basis of the systems in Canada (outside of Quebec), in Australia and New Zealand, in Trinidad and Barbados and the Bahamas, and in many other countries that were once part of the British empire. It is the core of the law in Nigeria and the Gambia and Singapore. But nobody outside this circle of English domination in fact has ever adopted the common law. In modern times, a number of non-Western countries have shopped around for a Western legal system, which (they thought) would do a better job of catapulting them into the contemporary world than their indigenous systems. Japan and Turkey are famous examples. In no case did such a country choose the American or English model. In every case, what was chosen was civil law, continental European law. Why? One answer is that these are *codified* systems. Their basic rules take the form of *codes*—rationally arranged mega-statutes, which set out the guts of the law, the essential concepts and doctrines. In theory, the judges have no power to add or subtract from the law, which is entirely contained within the codes. Their only task is to interpret these rules. The core of the common law, on the other hand, was essentially created by judges, as they decided actual cases. The common law grew, shifted, evolved, changed prismatically, over the years, as it confronted real litigants, and real situations. But as a result, it became hard to find and to identify "the law." The common law was, in a way, everywhere and nowhere—it was an abstraction, scattered among thousands of pages of case reports. It was not, in short, packaged for export.

In a common law system, the judges who write the opinions are crucial and important figures. To be more precise, the law gets made by *appellate* judges: judges who hear cases appealed from decisions on the level of the trial court. At the trial court level, on the other hand, the common law judge plays a much more muted role than the civil law judge. The civil law judge handles much of the job of working up the case, preparing it, investigating the facts. All this, in a common law system, is handled by lawyers; and the judge at the trial acts as a kind of umpire (a powerful one, to be sure). In common law countries (certainly in the United States) judges are themselves lawyers (practicing lawyers) who are elected or appointed to the bench, very often because they have been politically active. Civil law judges are, on the contrary, civil servants. Judging is a career on its own; judges are almost never recruited from among practicing lawyers; rather, they are trained from the very start to be judges, and they rise and fall entirely within the judicial hierarchy. And they are *never* elected.

There are many other differences, big ones and little ones, between common law and civil law systems. There are differences in procedures, in institutions, and in substantive rules. On the whole, civil law systems lack a jury, for example. There is an argument, though, that the systems, in the contemporary world, are converging—drawing closer and closer together. One reason may be that legal practice is globalizing: more and more legal effort goes into international deals and other matters that cross borders. But the main reason is simply that legal systems reflect the societies in which they are embedded; and these societies are becoming more and more alike. European countries, the United States, Canada, Japan, Australia, and other countries, despite their differences, have huge commonalities as well, in society and law. Modernity is much of a muchness everywhere. An automobile is an automobile in Tokyo or Helsinki; a computer is a computer in Frankfurt or Singapore. All modern, developed countries have income tax systems, stock exchanges, international airports, tall buildings with elevators, and traffic jams. They all face issues of copyright, pollution, air traffic control, and bank regulation. Similar problems tend to generate similar solutions; and similar problems and solutions mean similar laws and legal systems. Also, the distinction between the "judge-made" common law and the codified civil law has lost a good deal of its relevance. The common law systems now have plenty of statutes and codes—shelf after shelf of them, in the typical law library. More and more of the work of common law judges consists of interpreting statutes passed by Congress or by state legislatures. And, conversely, the role of the judge in civil law countries is becoming a great deal more powerful—is coming, in some ways, to resemble the work of the common law judge. Many differences remain, to be sure—especially in the way lawyers tend to think, and the precise kind of jargon they use—but the odor of convergence is also fairly strong.

The common law family has many members; and each of them has, of course, its own special features. American law, which is our subject, has departed in many ways from the law of England, where the common law was born and raised. For one thing, the United States is a *federal* republic; it is made up of fifty states, each of which has its own legal system, with a national system sitting on top of or next to these. The states handle the great bulk of the country's legal affairs. They grant divorces, put burglars on trial, run the school systems, and make up traffic rules. If you sue somebody who owes you money, you go to state court; if you want a driver's license or a hunting license, you go to a state agency; if you organize a corporation, or want to open a pizza parlor, the papers and red tape belong to the state. It is the state that arrests you for drunk driving, or opens its courts for you to sue Acme Appliances for selling a defective refrigerator. Probably more than 90 percent of all lawsuits are state lawsuits. In the last century or so, as we shall see, federalism has frayed a good deal about the edges, but it retains a good deal of its vitality.

The fraying is because the federal role in the legal system has been steadily growing. The volume and importance of federal courts, statutes, regulations, and executive orders has been spiraling upward for a century or more. Congress is a powerful body, and the federal government, after all, has the atom bomb, which Wyoming or Delaware (fortunately) do not. Federal courts handle federal issues: issues arising under the Constitution, or under laws passed by Congress—the Social Security Act, the Internal Revenue Code (income tax), environmental protection laws, antidiscrimination laws, antitrust laws. They deal with bankruptcy and maritime affairs, and they also hear many cases between citizens of different states (so-called diversity cases). The principle that governs whether some legal task is state or federal is not always obvious. Wars and ambassadors, of course: but why is bankruptcy federal? Why is it that a contract, made in New York, to ship two tons of pencils to Florida by water, can end up in federal court?

The United States is not the only federal system in the common law world. Australia and Canada are also federal. Nor does the common law world have a monopoly on federalism—Switzerland and Germany are also federal systems. But the law of England and Wales is a single entity (Scotland has its own legal order). Federalism makes the legal system of the United States an extremely complicated beast—a beast with fifty separate heads, bodies, and tails. Of course, the state systems are (for the most part) fairly similar—they have a definite family resemblance to one another. But they are far from identical. Hence, there is no such thing, really, as an "American" lawyer; lawyers are licensed state by state. As far as New Hampshire is concerned, a member of the Vermont bar is just a layman who knows a lot about the law (though not necessarily New Hampshire law).

In fact, there are more than fifty systems within the territory controlled by the United States. The federal system can be counted as number fifty-one; and in addition, there is Puerto Rico with its special history, its Spanish language, and its civil law tradition; there is Guam, and the Virgin Islands; and there are also the legal systems of many of the native peoples who live inside American borders. The Navajo, for example, have a court system, headed by the Navajo Supreme Court, which sits, hears cases, and decides them according to the laws that govern the Navajo nation—including some specifically Navajo norms.

Another special feature of American law is *judicial review*. Since the late eighteenth century, we have had a written Constitution (something the British never had). Judicial review is the power of courts to measure, against the constitutional standard, what other branches of government do. The Supreme Court of the United States has told states they cannot segregate the schools; has told a president (Harry Truman) he had no power to seize steel mills in what the president claimed was an emergency; has told Congress it had no power to pass certain laws; has reviewed all sorts of actions by administrative agencies. The Supreme Court has ordered states to redraw their district lines, has told school districts what kind of financial system they must use, has ordered states to clean up their filthy, brutal prisons—the list goes on and on. Moreover, each state has its own Supreme Court,[2] and its own constitution; and the state Supreme Courts play more or less the same role inside the state that the Supreme Court of the United States plays outside. They measure the work of their legislatures, and their agencies, against the standard of the state constitution (as they see it).

This has been a brief sketch of judicial review as it now exists: a powerful weapon in the hands of judges, a power to monitor, control, and sometimes chasten every other branch of government. It was not always this way. Judicial review is as much a *cultural* as a structural fact. Courts used it rarely and gingerly for the first century of independence. Whether the Supreme Court had the power to review acts of Congress at all was only settled in the famous case of *Marbury v. Madison*, John Marshall's great decision of 1803.[3] Perhaps this case settled the issue; but in fact, the Supreme Court did not clearly act to strike down another act of Congress until more than fifty years later (it did review acts of the states). Not until the late nineteenth century did judicial review of legislation become a normal part of the life cycle of major legislation. And only then did it become part of America's political and legal culture. Or perhaps it would be more accurate to say that it stemmed *from* America's political and legal culture. It is a structural element, but one that responds to American rights consciousness, American individualism, American fear of concentrated power, American suspicion of centralization, and the American tradition of dispersed, fragmented government. In such a system, "lawsuits and courts provide," as Robert Kagan has put it, "nonstatist mechanisms through which individuals"—and groups—"can demand high standards of justice" (as they see it) from government.[4]

Both judicial review and federalism are formal, structural features of American law—and at the same time, deeply rooted, insofar as they are realities, in American legal culture.

Other aspects of American law are more subtle reflections of American legal culture. Indeed, American habits of legal behavior seem rather different from the habits of people who live in Italy or England or Japan. Americans, it is said, are more rights conscious than most citizens of other countries; more prone to sue for damages. They litigate more. Supposedly, they are less likely to settle their differences out of court, or simply swallow them, compared to people in other societies. How true this is—and how different—is a vexed and disputed research question. In general, we cannot understand American law without understanding American legal culture; and that culture is a theme that runs through this entire book.

In the United States, as in many other countries, there is a kind of pyramid of courts—high ones and low ones. If you sue somebody, on a contract for example, the case will go to a trial court. There may or may not be a jury; in some cases you have the right to ask for a jury, in other cases, not. In any event, the loser at the trial has the right to appeal to a higher court. In the states, the state Supreme Court is the final stop on the trip. In the federal courts, it is the United States Supreme Court. These top courts are important not only because they are the end of the line for any controversy but also because they generally publish their decisions, giving reasons why they decided as they did. These opinions, published in thick volumes of reports (and, today, available online), in a real sense make the law (or some aspects of it, at least). These cases are also the basic units of *study* in the common law system. Cases are what law students actually read in their classes; the common law mind instinctively reaches out for "the cases."

Of course, there is a lot more to the American legal system than these cases. After all, the overwhelming majority of cases are never appealed to a higher court—indeed, the overwhelming majority of controversies never get to the courts at all. And there is a huge amount of "law" that never gets talked about or discussed in appellate cases. There are thousands of rules, statutes, ordinances, regulations that never achieve this kind of attention. No class in law school talks about traffic law, for example. It is too humble and workaday for that. But much of the work of lawyers—much of the work of the government—is humble and workaday. Case law is interesting, important, and enlightening: but it is by no means the whole show.

Lawyers have a tendency—quite naturally—to treat law as more or less "autonomous," that is, as a kind of kingdom of its own. It has its own jargon. It has a tough, inner core, which (they feel) is resistant to change. Law moves slowly and sluggishly, like a snail, encased in its shell; it "lags" behind society. It goes at its own pace, answers to its own rules, responds to its own inner program. But, in my view, this autonomy is mostly an illusion. The reality is quite different. Law is, essentially, a product of society; and as society changes, so does its legal system. Feudal societies have feudal legal systems; socialist societies have socialist systems; tribal societies have tribal systems; capitalist societies have capitalist legal systems. How could it be otherwise?

Of course, the legal tradition, and the habits and thoughts of lawyers, do have an impact on society; influence does not travel entirely in one direction. And the legal system, especially in a society like the United States, is not something distant, removed, remote, the province entirely of specialists, like nuclear physics or higher mathematics. It sinks its roots into the culture. It helps to *create* that culture. After all, people tend to accept what they are used to. They live in societies they take for granted; society's norms, customs, habits of thought are like the air they breathe: vital but invisible. Americans, for example, find it hard to conceive of a system of criminal justice without a jury. There are even more fundamental ideas that they do not even see as legal ideas: private property, for example, or the right to enter into contracts, or the concepts of marriage or divorce or adoption of children.

The relationship between law and society is complex in a complex society. It is also unstable: it shifts over time. I like to use a parable to illustrate the relationship—roughly, at least. Imagine a community that lives on the banks of a swift and deep river. The only way across is by ferry, slow and cumbersome. The community demands a bridge; the citizens sign petitions, lobby, and put pressure on their government. Finally, the government yields, money is appropriated, and the bridge gets built. Once the bridge is in place, traffic moves swiftly back and forth across the bridge. The nature of the community changes. Now people can and do split their lives between the two sides of the river. Some live on one side and shop and work on the other; and vice versa. Many people cross the bridge every day. People come to think of the bridge as natural, inevitable—even as something they have a kind of *right* to have. The bridge affects their behavior, their way of thinking, their expectations, their way of life.

The legal system is something like the bridge. The bridge itself was not "autonomous"; it was entirely the product of a social demand. But once in place, it began to exert an influence on behavior and on attitudes. It became part of the world of the people who lived in that community. They ordered their lives in reference to the bridge. The bridge entered into their very thought processes. American law is very much of this nature: it is one of society's bridges.

The parable, of course, is far too simple to describe reality: at best, it is a stripped-down version of the way the legal system operates, and its relationship to society. The parable illustrates a basic point, but obviously leaves a lot out. One key point, only implicit in the parable, is that law expresses the distribution of *power*. It takes social energy and force to make law; or to enforce law, or to change law. The legal system of any society is a mirror that reflects, necessarily, the structure of power in that society. If we understood exactly and completely how the legal system of some society worked, we would also have insight into who counts in that society, who has the power and the influence and the authority; and who does not. A legal system is certainly not "the will of the people." This is completely obvious in a society like Hitler's Germany or any dictatorship or authoritarian society. In such a society, what the law represents, most of all, is the will and the needs and the aspirations of the ruler and his immediate circle; and perhaps other people and institutions of power.

But we live in a more or less democratic society, and the way law relates to power is much more subtle than in a place like Hitler's Germany. "The people" obviously count for much more. Still, you would have to be very naive not to realize that wealth and power profoundly influence the making and execution of the laws. The legal system expresses, in word and deed, the dominant norms and the ruling ideas. This is not the same as saying that big corporations and rich people run the country. Big corporations and rich people make a mark on the system, of course. But so does the vast middle class. What the middle class thinks and feels about property, marriage and divorce, sexual behavior, lawsuits for accidents, the right to sue HMOs, and countless other subjects, can be decisive. As norms change, so do the laws.

In addition, the legal order also expresses *limits* on power. This is most obvious in the constitutional scheme—in the Bill of Rights and the gloss that the courts have put on it. Minorities and common folk are protected (one hopes) in some basic regards from the tyranny of the majority or the tyranny of the rich and mighty. How much protection, and how far it goes, is a much debated question. But clearly the law expresses values and ideals as well as power; and clearly these values and ideals seep into the consciousness of citizens, high and low, and affect the way they behave, the policies they pursue, the candidates they vote for. Behavior and attitudes are affected; but how much is hard to tell.

Law is, after all, not simply authority; it is authority that carries with it a stamp of *legitimacy*. It is part of the nature of law to base its authority on something other than naked power. Might may make right; but might has to be careful not to make this fact too obvious. And it is hard to run a society *only* through terror and force. Dictatorships, especially in the contemporary world, are inherently unstable.

Where does legitimacy come from? What gives a rule or an institution legitimate authority?[5] This varies from society to society. In many societies, people believe that the rules come from a source outside any human authority: from God, or his prophets. This is the legitimacy of the rules of the Bible, for example. Many systems still make this claim: Iran and Afghanistan, to name two instances, claim to rest much of their law on holy, timeless Koranic principles. But in modern democratic systems, legitimacy is more a matter of procedure. The laws are man-made and instrumental; and what legitimates them, on the whole, is the fact that they come from a legislature elected by popular vote. Majority rule, in short, legitimates the enacted laws; a majority of the voters, and then a majority of congressmen or senators. Other rules are legitimate because they are embedded in a constitution or rest on some constitutional text that, in a more or less vague way, was ratified and continues to be ratified by some sort of social consensus. And still other norms gain their power because people believe that they are "inherent," that everybody is entitled to them, whether or not a legislature ever said yes or said no. As these ideas rattle about in the heads of ordinary citizens, they influence attitudes, and hence behavior, and hence law—whether or not the ideas make sense, whether they are consistent or inconsistent, coherent or incoherent. Ordinary people, big and small, are not philosophers. They are . . . people. What counts in norms is their strength, how deeply rooted they are, how strongly held; when they are strong enough, they act as pillars holding up the system, preventing it from collapsing into anarchy and revolution.

NOTES

1. For a concise overview, see John Henry Merryman, *The Civil Law Tradition: An Introduction to the Legal Systems of Western Europe and Latin America* (2d ed., 1985).

2. Not always called a Supreme Court: the highest court in New York state is called the Court of Appeals. The Supreme Court in New York is actually one of the lowest courts—illogical as the terminology may seem.

3. 1 Cranch (5 U.S.) 137 (1803).

4. Robert A. Kagan, *Adversarial Legalism: The American Way of Law* (2001), pp. 15–16.

5. The classic treatment of this subject, of course, is Max Weber's; see Max Rheinstein, ed., *Max Weber on Law in Economy and Society* (1954); see also Tom R. Tyler, *Why People Obey the Law* (1990).

TWO

IN THE BEGINNING: AMERICAN LAW IN THE COLONIAL PERIOD

The English began to settle what is now the United States at the beginning of the seventeenth century. They founded colonies all up and down the coast, from what we now call Maine to Georgia. (They also colonized parts of what is now Canada; and many of the Caribbean islands.) The period up to 1776 is called the colonial period; and we give these settlements the name of colonies. But they were not like, say, the British colonies in the nineteenth century. Many of the American colonies were, for all intents and purposes, independent. Some of them were almost the private property of "proprietors," who had gotten grants of vast lands from the Crown. Other colonies were in effect self-governing—in practice, if not in theory. This was true, for example, of Massachusetts Bay. In all cases, English control was extremely weak. England was very far away—a long, arduous, and dangerous trip by water; and England had no real colonial policy, at least not to begin with. England had neither the opportunity nor the skill nor the experience to manage an "empire."

The colonial communities were small and poor; in the early days, some of them came close to starving. They were rich only in one commodity, land. Labor was in short supply. Climate was an important influence on the colonies—the further south one went, the warmer it got, and, with longer growing seasons, it was easier to develop large-scale agriculture. In addition, some of the New England colonies were founded by Puritans, and Protestant clergymen had enormous influence over life and law in these colonies. The southern colonies were somewhat closer to English models in both law and ways of life. In the south, there were fewer towns and cities; and the southern colonies soon became bastions of plantation agriculture, growing crops like tobacco and cotton; they also developed the "peculiar institution" of slavery (more on this later).

What was the law of the colonial period like? In essence, it was English law—at least in the sense that this was the only system the colonists knew anything about. They were used to it, and they brought with them their (lay) ideas and memories of legal practices; it was as natural to them as their American speech. If you look at the records of colonial courts, you find them bristling with legal terms (not always used correctly, by English standards). But some of these terms, like court, judge, jury, plaintiff, defendant, last will, are nothing more than ordinary English—part of everyday life. Of course, in their tiny settlements, and before there were many lawyers around, the law that the colonies followed was fairly crude and stripped down, from the English standpoint at least. English law was the law of an older society, with a strong feudal past, and an elaborate and complex social system, starting with the king on top, and down through layers of aristocracy and gentry to the common folk. Most of the maddening complexity of English law, highly crabbed and technical, was not only unknown in the colonies; it was also unnecessary. The colonists took what they knew, what they needed, what they remembered.

As the colonies grew, and when such towns as Boston became important ports and commercial centers, the law became somewhat more sophisticated; but it never reached the heights (or depths) of English law. The colonists also adapted, changed, and added to the law, in ways that suited their situation, which was, after all, very different from the situation of the ordinary English man or woman. Also, the ideologies of the colonists shaped their laws in important ways. The Puritans in Massachusetts, for example, made law to suit their idea of a godly society. They had rules about heretics, blasphemy, church attendance, and, above all, about moral behavior (more on this later too).

We know a lot about the law of Massachusetts Bay in the seventeenth century from surviving records. We know a lot about society in that period, too. The communities were small, tight-knit, hierarchical. Some of the settlements were small enough so that probably everybody knew everybody else. The leading citizens were the clergy, and the (male) heads of household. At the bottom of the social ladder were slaves and indentured servants. Every colony, including Massachusetts, had black slaves; but the numbers increased as you went from north to south. Indentured servants were mostly white; an indentured servant was a kind of temporary slave. He or she served a master and mistress, without pay, for a period of years, usually living in the household. Many immigrants offered themselves for sale in this way, to get the money for their passage. Indentured servants could not quit their job before their time was up; an indentured servant could not marry without the permission of the master; and the master could buy and sell the servant, just as a slave could be bought and sold. But at the end of their term, servants, unlike slaves, became free. Sometimes they also received "freedom dues." A Maryland law of 1640 made the master provide a male servant whose time was up with a shirt, shoes and stockings, a cap, two hoes, an ax, three barrels of corn, and fifty acres of land; women received "freedom dues" as well.[1]

Massachusetts developed its own elaborate system of courts. At the top was the General Court, under it a Court of Assistants. Local courts handled day-to-day issues; they also handled a lot of what we would now call administrative work—they registered brand marks of cattle, for example, laid down rules, recorded wills and land documents, and so on. The idea of the separation of powers was not to be found in the colonies. The courts acted, as it were, as full-service government stations. And the law played an important role in the everyday life of the community. Almost everybody—certainly almost every adult—in a small community was bound to find his or her way into the court records, in one form or another, during any particular year. The court records, in some ways, are mirrors of the whole life of the community.

The laws of the colonies were, as we said, basically English, but a stripped-down version. Much of what we think of as English law—the law reflected in the sourcebooks—is really a law about the problems of the landed aristocracy. But there was no landed aristocracy in the colonies—certainly not in the northern colonies. It was a more popular, local kind of law that took hold on this side of the Atlantic. "Popular" here does not mean democratic (as we understand the word). It would be more accurate to call the colonies little theocracies. But they were popular in other senses. Courts were right at everybody's doorstep in these small communities. And they dealt with matters that concerned everybody, as we said.

Colonial law also included a number of quite striking innovations. The first, which nobody is proud of today, was the law of slavery. Slavery was unknown to England, and to English law. There was slavery in the colonies in the seventeenth century; some Indians were enslaved, but on the whole, slavery was always closely associated with black men and women brought from Africa. There is controversy over where slavery came from, and how it got started; clearly it began as a kind of custom, a general understanding, before it was ever formalized as "law," that is, as a recognized legal status. As early as the 1620s, there was some *suggestion* that the colonies already recognized a custom of treating at least some black servants as slaves. The evidence comes from lists of names, in which last names were left off, from valuations in inventories of estates, and the like. Also, there was slavery in the Portuguese and Spanish colonies in the sixteenth century; and slavery developed in the sugar colonies of the West Indies; the first settlers in Barbados, in 1627, brought with them ten blacks; and in 1636, in Barbados, there was already discussion of "slaves for life." In Virginia, there were blacks as early as 1619; and in 1640, the first evidence of the *legal* status of slavery appears. By the middle of the seventeenth century, there are scattered references in the records that strongly suggest a custom of lifetime servitude—"servants" who would never go free; these "servants" were invariably black. Shortly thereafter, the law recognized the other essential element of slavery: that children of slave mothers were themselves doomed to be slaves.

There is no question that a strong consciousness of *race* was a crucial element driving the laws and customs of slavery. True, many white people were also unfree—they were indentured servants, which, as we have seen, was a kind of temporary slavery; but permanent, lifetime, inherited slavery never applied to white people, only to black people, imported from Africa. There was enslavement of Indians, too; but this system did not last. The Indians, after all, were in a different position. This was their country; they could be a threat to the settlers; it was important not to alienate them; and, perhaps most important, they had a hinterland to escape to; for black Africans, this was not usually possible. The natives also formed compact language and culture groups; the blacks were drawn from dozens of distinct African language and culture groups, and the process of enslavement essentially detribalized them, mixing them into a single subordinate mass. There are interesting survivals of African customs, names, and languages—in the Gullah dialect, for example—and perhaps in other aspects of slave life. But the conditions of slavery tended to wipe out the cultures these men and women brought with them. They also were converted to Christianity—

though the law made it plain that conversion did not set a slave free.

The slaves were of course important for the economy. They were used in the sugar plantations of the West Indies as well as on the plantations of the American south. In the colonies, there was always a severe shortage of labor. Blacks were imported from Africa to do the hard work in the fields. Slavery was well known in Africa, and the slave trade depended on African help in enslaving other Africans. Blacks were kidnapped or captured in Africa, loaded on ships, and transported (under terrible conditions) to the colonies. Culturally and racially, blacks were extremely different from the whites who lived in the colonies. The deep consciousness of race—America's original sin—helped to bind these foreign servants to a status that degraded and exploited them. For whites, it was unthinkable that blacks would simply serve a term of years and then start climbing the ladder of mobility. There *were* free blacks, and black servants. They were never treated as equals to the whites. And, more and more, the preferred and dominant status was the status of a slave.

There has been something of a debate about the differences between slavery in British America and in Latin America. Some argue that British American slavery was much harsher. The claim is that Latin America treated freed slaves much like nonslaves, and that the humanity of slaves was recognized—they were, for example, allowed to marry. In America, free blacks (blacks who had never been slaves, or who had been set free) were never full citizens, and slaves were not allowed (legally) to marry (there were, of course, couples who lived together as man and wife, and treated each other as such). It does seem clear that the sheer element of *race* counted very heavily—was more central—in the British colonies compared to Latin America. There caste, shade of color, culture, position in society counted far more. In what became America, a black was a black was a black; and even a slight admixture of black blood made you legally black. After all, slave women often gave birth to children of white owners and overseers; and in time, there were slaves on some plantations whose skin was almost white.

In any event, the slave population became more and more significant, economically and socially, in the southern colonies. In Virginia, in 1649, blacks made up about 2 percent of the population. By 1750, they constituted about 40 percent of the population—and the overwhelming majority of these were slaves. By this time, too, Virginia, and the other colonies, had built up an enormous body of slave *law*. The law played an important part in making the institution strong, clear, and permanent. The law codified custom and crystallized it; it put its enforcement power behind the "peculiar institution." People who, later on, opposed slavery were deviants, as far as southern culture and ideology was concerned; the law, in fact, made every attempt to buttress slavery. Slave law grew up out of custom—but once in place, it constrained both thought and action. This, indeed, is one of the ways in which law makes itself felt in society: it takes an understanding, a norm, an attitude, and it hardens it into muscle and bone.

Politics, in the southern colonies, was dominated by the landed gentry, who typically owned whole gangs of slaves. Southern colonies for example placed restrictions on manumission—they made it harder to set slaves free. As the years went on, an elaborate slave code was created. It enforced the race and caste aspects of slavery. The code—different in each colony, of course, but with strong family resemblances—was made up of three main aspects. There were rules about the status of the slaves: rules that made it unlawful for them to own property, marry, buy and sell—rules that defined their status as human beings who were owned as if they were dogs or cattle, and could be bought and sold and rented. Then there were rules relating to the social control of slaves, rules allowing the master to punish his slaves, ordering slaves to obey, and punishing slaves who ran away or who rose up against their owners. Then there was also a vast body of very technical law about slavery, just as there was and is a vast body of quite technical law about real estate, oil and gas, water rights, patents, and other forms of property: the commercial law, as it were, of black Americans who were held as chattels.

This huge body of law, with no real equivalent in the mother country, is an embarrassment to Americans today (or should be); but there were other, less embarrassing innovations in colonial law. In some ways, colonial America was a vast natural experiment: it tested what happened to the common law when it was yanked out of its socket and transported to a new place, a kind of wilderness, where the English settlers could make a fresh start, and where the encrusted social structure of England had no chance to take root. What one finds is that the law underwent a sea change. In England, for example, the land was closely held by great families in their stately country homes; the dominant rule in land inheritance was primogeniture: the land went to the "heir," that is, the oldest son. To some extent, this continued to be the case in the southern colonies, with their large estates worked by black field hands. But the northern colonies, where the dominant form of land tenure was what we would now call the family farm, abandoned primogeniture. There was plenty of land, and no real felt need to keep "estates" intact, and in the hands of a single heir. The northern rule, therefore, was so-called *partible* inheritance: the land was (for the most part) divided equally among the children, although in Massachusetts for a while, the oldest son got a double share.

In England, a tiny percentage of the population—1 or 2 percent at most—owned almost all of the land. But in New

England, there were no great landlords, no great estates. Land was, or seemed to be, available for everybody. Of course, there were the native tribes; but the white settlers never really understood them, or their relationship to the land. The impact on the law of this simple, brute fact, the abundance of land, the widespread ownership of land, was incalculable.

In short, a system of law grew up on the west shore of the Atlantic, which was very much its own creation, even though it was obviously related to the law of mother England. Perhaps we should say *systems* of laws, because each colony had its own peculiarities. To be sure, as the population grew, and the towns turned into cities, there was a certain approximation to English law; this was particularly significant in fields of commercial law. The English were the most important trading partners, after all. Moreover, the colonies were poor in legal sources; few law books were published in the colonies, and lawyers and judges relied very much on English materials (not that these were themselves at all common in the colonies). William Blackstone's *Commentaries on the Laws of England,* published in the middle of the eighteenth century, became a wild best-seller in legal circles on the American side of the Atlantic. Here, in limpid and elegant English, and in the short space of four volumes, was a skeleton key to the mysteries of English law: a guide to its basic substance.

Most of the historical interest in the eighteenth century has focused on the independence movement. This was of course a complex process; resentment grew as British rule tightened and became more genuinely imperial. But the cultural roots of the Revolution are perhaps even more significant. The Americans had simply grown apart from the British. They had developed a social system that fit very badly with the government of King George III. Despite slavery, indentured servitude, and the usual distinctions between rich and poor, American society was a lot more egalitarian than English society. This was, in large part, because the *conditions* in the colonies were so different from the conditions in the old country. This was frontier country, with an abundance of land. New England in particular was organized, not on the basis of a landed aristocracy, but, as we saw, on the basis of family farms. Besides, England was remote, as we said, and few Americans born on this side of the Atlantic had ever been there. Loyalty to the Crown would have been a little much to ask.

The colonies won independence after a long war; but unlike say the French or the Russian revolutions, there was no sharp *legal* break with the past. The common law system (American style) remained intact. Indeed, in some sense, the aim of the Revolution was continuity, not overthrow: continuity of the colonial traditions, laws, and ways of life. For the most part, the British had left the colonies more or less alone. In the beginning, they pretty much had to: the ocean was a tremendous barrier to communication; and to governance as well. When the British woke up to the fact of empire, and tried to assert some control over their restless children, it turned out to be already too late.

After the war, the former colonists set about to create an independent republic. There was to be no king. There were to be no nobles, no aristocracy. Allegiance would go, not to a man with a crown, but to the law, or to the idea of law. It was to be a "government of laws and not of men." This expresses an ideal that was the basis for the experiment in democracy— or at least in democracy as defined by the leading men of the time. Like many ideals, the notion of a government "of laws" can never be reached (and perhaps *shouldn't* be reached); in this society, as in every society, who you know and what your connections are, whether you are rich or poor, educated or uneducated, articulate or inarticulate, has always mattered greatly—one way or the other. But compared to the royal government of England of the late eighteenth century—and continental governments even more so—the American experiment was indeed a society based more on laws, rules, general principles, than on royal prerogatives, and the divine right of nobles and bishops.

Building a new plan of government—stitching together a framework that all the colonies could agree on—was far from easy. The first plan, the Articles of Confederation, provided for a weak central government. When this failed to work out, a convention met and proposed a federal constitution, which was duly adopted and went into effect. Great Britain had and has no written constitution. But the colonies, with their charters and compacts, were used to the idea of operating under some sort of fundamental text. The constitution they drafted was the first and only constitution of the United States. It is still with us today—the world's oldest living constitution—and the text has not changed radically. Ratifying the Constitution was a struggle; one complaint was that the text lacked a bill of rights. To meet this objection, ten amendments—the Bill of Rights—were adopted almost immediately. Since then, the Constitution has been amended very little. Some of the amendments—the Fourteenth, for example—have been enormously important. The total number has been twenty-seven.

The Constitution set out the basic frame of government—president, Congress, Supreme Court, a federal system—and laid down a few fundamental rules. It is comparatively short and sweet. A few of its provisions are quite specific—the president has to be at least thirty-five years old—but others are broad and malleable. Perhaps the Constitution has lasted so long, and served the country so well, because it is brief and general—helped by the fact that it acquired, very soon, a kind of aura of the sacred. Each of the states eventually adopted a constitution of its own. But these have been much less stable.

The earliest state constitutions are earlier than the federal Constitution, and had some influence on it. Since then, the influence has flowed the other way. Each state constitution more or less follows the general *pattern* of the federal Constitution. They all set out the basic scheme of the state government. They all contain a bill of rights. But they are much more brittle than the federal Constitution—and they lack its charisma entirely. Some states have made do with a single constitution; others have molted them from time to time. Louisiana, the champion, has had ten or eleven constitutions, depending on how one counts. The state constitutions are also amended much more frequently than the federal Constitution. Here the champion seems to be the current Georgia constitution, with over 650 amendments.

NOTE

1. Clifford Lindsey Alderman, *Colonists for Sale: The Story of Indentured Servants in America* (1975), pp. 74–75.

THREE

ECONOMY AND LAW IN THE NINETEENTH CENTURY

The general idea behind this book is that American law is a reflection of what goes on in American society in general. The reflection may not be exact: it may be like the reflection of a face in a slowly moving river, that is, somewhat refracted and distorted. But it is a reflection nonetheless. In this chapter, we will look at this relationship between law and society in one critical area, law and the economy—that is, law and the business of making a living and distributing goods and services in society.

ECONOMY

Most people think of the nineteenth century as the age of laissez-faire, a period in which government did as little as possible. The economy was left to function on its own. The free market ruled. There is a lot of truth to this, but it is not the truth, the whole truth, and nothing but the truth. In fact, government and law had a critical role in the economy. Some aspects of that role were basic, so basic that people tended to take them for granted. They took for granted, for example, the idea of private property—in land, in commodities of all sorts. They took for granted the institution of *contract:* the right to buy and sell, to make agreements, with the understanding that the force of law stood behind these agreements.

Government intervened in the economy, or supported it, in other ways as well. Of course, when we say "government," we are not thinking of the huge Leviathan of today—a national government that raises billions and billions of dollars and has millions of employees; and state governments that are of enormous size on their own. The budget of a medium-sized city—Wichita, or Milwaukee, or Birmingham—is undoubtedly bigger than the whole national budget in the early nineteenth century. It is important to debunk the myth of total laissez-faire; but once this is done, it is equally important to see that the role of law and government in the nineteenth century was very different from what it is today.

Undoubtedly, the early nineteenth century was a boom time. Or, more accurately, boom and bust; but the booms outweighed the busts. The gross national product rose steadily during the period. Agriculture was still the main business of Americans; but manufacturing was already coming on strong in the first half of the century. Population was growing rapidly as well—the three millions of 1790 had grown to 31.4 millions by 1860. Much of this growth was due to immigration: 8,000 people entered the country in 1820, 369,000 in 1850.

What activities of the citizen were subject to legal, state-enforced rules in this period, and which were not? What spheres were "free" and which were not? And, perhaps most important, what did it *feel* like? Did people *feel* free? Freedom is not an absolute; it is something relative, and it is also quite subjective. Consider, for example, that twentieth-century miracle, the automobile. Now that most people have cars, they have opportunities that were denied most people in the past. They can live, work, travel in ways that expand their horizons. In this sense, the automobile makes an enormous contribution to "freedom"; it carries the priceless gift of mobility. It provides a kind of "freedom" that the nineteenth century could hardly dream of. Yet the automobile also generates a tremendous volume of law—a mass of rules about roads, traffic, driver's licenses, all of which regulate and restrict and set limits. You never needed a walker's license to walk, or a rider's license to ride a horse, or to pull a cart. Do these automobile rules mean that people are less free today than they were before the age of the automobile? This question is impossible to answer; but one thing is clear, the mere fact that people are subject to more *rules,* more *law,* does not make them less free. In any event, it is hard to compare across centuries. Nobody in 1850 had a telephone; it was not part of the market basket of goods. Nobody in 1900 could travel across the country by airplane. Nobody in 1920 had a computer. But nobody feels the lack of something that doesn't yet exist.

In any event, in the nineteenth century, law-government was much more peripheral than it is today; and government did much less regulating. Its main aim was *promotional;* to enact laws to help the economy grow. This seems banal—today, it seems perfectly clear that this is something a government should do. It has a duty to promote the economy, do something perhaps about unemployment or the business cycle, or the money supply. But it was far from obvious in the past. The feudal kings had no such notion. They were mostly out for themselves. "Promotion," or, in the trenchant phrase of Willard Hurst, a noted legal historian, the "release of energy," is tied closely to the idea of progress—the idea that history is marching in a particular direction; that things are supposed to get better, richer, more modern, more complex.

In any event, regulation, though mostly promotion, was greater than most people imagine. William Novak, in his book *The People's Welfare,* has explored a world largely lost to our view. This is the nineteenth-century world of governmental action—the many rules and regulations about quarantines, safety, use of land, and the like, mostly on the level of the states, during the course of the nineteenth century. And the states were where most of the action was—the states and the cities. The health regulations of New York City in 1860 were numerous enough to fill a whole volume. The Sanitary Code, by 1872, had 181 provisions, dealing with everything from alcoholic spirits through "yarding cattle."[1] Today we tend to look at government regulation from the lens of Washington, D.C., and the national Congress and president. Washington is the central city of a huge metropolitan area. It is full of huge, imposing buildings of marble and stone, home to the great agencies and departments. But in the nineteenth century Washington was a muddy, humid village. Members of the Supreme Court, for example, never lived there; they came, stayed in boarding houses, did their business, and went home as soon as they could. The bureaucracy was tiny. Nobody expected much out of the central government—or wanted much. The national government was like the brain of a dinosaur: an insignificant mass of neurons inside a gigantic body.

What did government—state and national—do to promote the economy? Some things were completely basic: a functioning court system, protection of property rights. Beyond this, government was concerned above all with creation of *infrastructure:* with those institutions that made economic growth possible. You cannot get goods to market without roads, canals, bridges, ferries, and (later) railroads. You cannot open up new country and settle the west without paths through the wilderness. Then there is the invisible infrastructure: money, credit, banks. How much the government should go into the banking business, or regulate it, was a matter of controversy; especially on issues of national banking. But there was less argument over helping build pathways for people and goods. There was heavy government aid to canals, turnpikes, and the like. The national government had very little in the way of money, but it had land to burn. It used land grants to stimulate the economy—grants to states for educational purposes, cheap land to settlers. The national government also gave away land that was worthless in its present state, to those who would put it to productive use. For example, a law of 1850 granted to the State of Arkansas all the "swamp and overflowed lands" that were "unfit . . . for cultivation." The state was to sell the land and use the proceeds to "construct the necessary levees and drains." The act gave the same privilege to other states with swamp lands.[2] Ultimately, almost 64 million acres were turned over to the states.[3] In general, the vast treasury of land was to be used, not primarily to raise money (though this was certainly not ignored), but to help develop the land, to help get it into the hands of people who would make it productive. The government also used land grants as rewards for service—the very next statute in the federal statute book, after the swamp land act, granted land to widows and children of "deceased . . . officers, musicians, or privates," who served in the War of 1812, or the "Indian wars," or the war with Mexico. For those who served nine months or more, the grant was 160 acres; for those who served less, there were lesser amounts.[4]

But above all, land grants and other subsidies went to build railroads, canals, and turnpikes. State and local governments floated bonds to help in construction; some states actually bought stock in railroads, all states tried in all sorts of ways to stimulate networks of communication. The Panic of 1837, one of the periodic calamities that overtook the economy, was something of a turning point; it soured many states on the whole idea of investing state money in private businesses, or in owning or running railroads. Five states defaulted on interest payments. After 1842, many states, including Ohio and Illinois, passed laws to forbid the state from lending money to enterprises of internal improvement; Michigan, Indiana, Ohio, Iowa prohibited the state from owning stock in companies. Pennsylvania and Tennessee abandoned their programs and sold off their interests in businesses. Experiments with state ownership of railroads came to a screeching halt. The national government, on the other hand, did not give up on the idea of helping private promoters of railroads; later in the century, it gave out thousands and thousands of acres, to help build up a railroad net. It granted land to promoters who promised to build railroads across the arid, forbidding wastes that separated the middle west from California and Oregon. The idea was that the promoters would sell the land, and use the proceeds to finance the roads.

The states tried to support enterprises in a variety of ways. For example, up until 1830, lotteries were commonly used. There also was a good deal of foreign investment—chiefly French and English. Then there was the law itself. This is a more difficult and subtle proposition—and one on which all scholars do not agree. If a state passes a law giving money to a railroad, that is a fairly obvious way of supporting the enterprise. It is much less obvious if a court shifts a doctrine slightly, or casts an old principle in a new light—and the net result is to tilt the scales a bit more toward the needs or wants of an enterprise. If this happens often enough, it can hardly be random or accidental. On the other hand, it need not be conscious, cold-blooded policy—American law was strongly pro-enterprise, but I suspect that most judges thought they were simply doing the right thing, and even the legal thing. They were men of their times, and they were responding to the norms of their times—to the hidden voices of the zeitgeist.

The early nineteenth century made a sharp distinction—not always explicitly—between property that was put to productive use and property that was lying fallow or was unproductive. People distinguished between "monopolists" and land speculators (who simply bought land and held it waiting for a rise in land values); and the good citizens who cleared land, built houses or stores, planted crops, or in some other way made the land productive. In a way, it is a conception of property "in motion" as opposed to property at rest.

Policy favored *dynamic* property, not static property. English law had had the habit of protecting vested rights—in particular, the rights of those men and women who owned great landed estates. American law took a sharp turn away from this position. The laws strongly favored doers, not holders; the active farmers, merchants, builders of roads and canals, not men who simply owned or held on to property.

One can make a similar point about the development of the law of *negligence*. The law of torts was one of the great growth fields of the nineteenth century. Torts are "civil wrongs," as opposed to criminal wrongs. The state prosecutes people who do criminal wrongs. Private individuals can sue for damages, against a "tortfeasor," that is, someone who has done them a noncriminal wrong. The law of torts is a sort of ragbag—it includes actions for libel and slander, trespass to property, and a number of other (minor) infractions of good order. But the vast majority of tort actions, from the nineteenth century on, were actions for "negligence," actions that came out of accidents, in which the plaintiff complained about some action that injured his body or his property. Actions of this sort are as old as Hammurabi and probably older; but they never amounted to a significant part of the law until the Industrial Revolution. Nothing does a better job of mangling human bodies than machines. Railroad locomotives, belching fire and steam, and racing through the countryside, were a tremendous source of injuries and deaths. They were among the earliest of the truly deadly machines. The steamboat was another. Steamboat boilers caused terrible injuries, as they exploded on board the boats; these calamities burned, scalded, and drowned victims by the hundreds. The explosion on the *Sultana,* a sidewheel steamboat, on April 27, 1865, killed more than 1,700 people—most of them former prisoners of war, on their way home from southern prison camps.[5]

Victims, under nineteenth-century doctrine, could recover

if they could show that the railroad or steamboat company was "negligent." This meant proving, in some way, that the defendant did not live up to the reasonable and normal standard of care. In a way, it seems illogical to force the plaintiff to prove the defendant was negligent. If X does something that breaks Y's bones, the loss is going to fall either on X or on Y. Since, after all, X did whatever it was that caused the loss, why not make him pay, rather than let poor Y bear the burden. This is certainly one possible way of handling the situation—this would be called "absolute liability." It is exactly what the law did in the case of freight. If I shipped packages on a railroad, and the goods were lost in a wreck, the railroad would simply have to pay; and it would be no defense at all for the railroad to argue that it was not "negligent." But if a *person* died in the same wreck, or lost an eye or a leg, that person or his family could not get a cent out of the railroad unless they could show that the railroad was "at fault," or careless in some way. The upshot was to insulate the railroad from liability, except when the passenger could show that some norm of safety had been violated. And there was also in the background the idea that accidents do happen, that enterprises inevitably cause harm—you can't make an omelette without breaking eggs—and that this was the price of progress.

It is often said that there was a shift from strict liability to a moralistic "fault" principle in the first half of the nineteenth century. There was, in fact, a fault principle, but it was hardly moralistic. It was not a question of morality at all, but a question of where to place risks of loss. And it is not really accurate to talk about a shift from strict liability; rather, there was a shift from *no* liability—from an absence of rules and cases—to a period in which tort cases sprouted like weeds between the cracks of an emerging industrial system. It was no surprise that the law favored railroads and other entrepreneurs.

The defendants in negligence cases—railroads for example—were those who were "in motion," in a manner of speaking, rather than those who were at rest (metaphorically, anyway: railroad passengers were certainly moving pretty fast). The defendants were the entrepreneurs, the doers, the bringers of wealth. And the law tilted toward these people, as opposed to the ordinary citizen. Was this because of the influence of the wealthy and powerful? Possibly; but in this period, quite ordinary people—farmers, for example—were desperately anxious for railroads to get built, and eager for them to prosper. The railroads were their lifeline to the market. They needed some way to move their produce to the cities. The developmental thrust of American law was thus everywhere in the law. It showed itself in the rules that favored railroads. It showed itself in tort law in general. It showed itself in land law, and in attitudes toward the public domain. It was, in short, almost ubiquitous.

In *Farwell v. Boston & Worcester Railroad Co.*, a Massachusetts case from 1842,[6] a railroad employee named Nicholas Farwell suffered a terrible injury on the job. Farwell was a railroad engineer; one day, a switchman allowed a train to run off the track; Farwell was thrown to the ground, and a wheel of the car crushed his hand. He sued the railroad, claiming that the negligence of another worker was the cause of his injury. It was a new kind of case (a case of "first impression") in Massachusetts. But Farwell's lawsuit rested itself on an old, established principle: if an agent (a servant or employee), on the job, does something that harms somebody else, that somebody could sue the principal (the master or employer), because the principal is generally responsible for acts of the agent. As an old maxim put it, what you do through somebody else is as if you did it yourself. The only wrinkle in the *Farwell* case was that *both* the man who did the damage and the man who suffered the harm were employees of a single company. The judge, Lemuel Shaw (one of the most able judges of the first half of the century and, incidentally, Herman Melville's father-in-law), refused to allow Farwell's claim. There was skimpy precedent—one English case; and a case from South Carolina.[7] But Shaw was not terribly interested in precedent—at least not in this particular instance. He felt that Farwell's agreement with the railroad, his wage contract (at $2 a day), included a kind of premium for dangerous work—otherwise (Shaw felt) the pay would be less. In any event, the case established the so-called fellow servant rule: in essence, that one employee could not sue the employer if the injury was the result of the negligence of a fellow employee (a "fellow servant"). Other states soon climbed on this particular bandwagon. The result was, in effect, to insulate entrepreneurs from injury claims brought by their workers. As for maimed or mangled railroad workers, well, they would have to shift for themselves.

To the modern reader, this seems incredibly callous. Especially so, in that there was no social safety net to speak of: no government programs of relief, unemployment, health insurance, and so on. Private insurance hardly existed; and in any event, men like Nicholas Farwell could not afford it. Public charity was the poorhouse: miserable, stingy, regimented, degrading, and almost as bad as imprisonment. Farwell and his family almost certainly faced a bitter and wretched future, unless family or friends or a church could come to the rescue. But the lack of a social safety net, paradoxically, makes the case less callous than it seems. Life was cruel and capricious—in general. The farmer, the merchant, the laborer—all were at the mercy of chance calamities, crops destroyed by weather, banks that failed, ships that sank, diseases that struck down breadwinners. Noncompensation was the general rule, not the exception. What happened to Farwell was, in Shaw's words, an "accident," that is, a chance event, bad luck, something that simply occurs; and accidents, like the one that befell Nicholas Farwell, were the common fate of thousands of women and men in all societies. Accidents must rest, as Shaw put it, where they first fell. In this case, the accident first fell on poor Nicholas.

When we come to judge the case, we should also remember that most people, at the time, were not landless workers, workers in factories and railroads, like Nicholas Farwell. Most people were farmers or lived on farms, or in small towns, and they desperately wanted railroads to be built, as we said. At the time of the *Farwell* case, it was most definitely in the interests of farmers, small merchants, and almost everybody to stimulate enterprise, and particularly railroads. Once the investments were made, and there was a fully functioning railroad net, the situation altered, and attitudes changed dramatically. The railroads, in one short generation, became villains, the octopus, the dreaded monopoly that held the farmer and the small merchant in its iron grip. But that story lay in the future.

The *Farwell* case, and others like it, tilted the scales of the law toward enterprise—toward railroads, in particular. What lay behind this decision? Were Shaw and the other judges simply following "the law"? Was their decision based on traditional legal principles and logic? It is hard to make this argument. For one thing, as Shaw himself admitted, it was a new case, one that had never come up before in Massachusetts. Was his decision a conscious attempt to help out the railroads? Shaw was, after all, a shrewd judge, supremely intelligent, and aware of the consequences of his acts. Did he set out, deliberately, to "subsidize" the railroads with rules slanted in their direction? This sounds, on the whole, too calculating. Of course, it is impossible to read a judge's mind. And legal opinions are much too formal, too opaque to tell us what goes on underneath the surface. What does seem clear is that the prevailing ethos of the times favored rapid growth, enterprise, the release of creative (economic) energy;[8] and judges, who are human beings of their times, pushed consciously or unconsciously in the policy direction that the spirit of the age made them comfortable with. Whatever Shaw had in his conscious or subconscious mind, the decision was in line with the flow of doctrine in the first half of the century: it favored enterprise, especially the railroads, and gave them what Shaw must have felt was some sort of protection from the dangers of accident litigation.

The period between the Revolution and the Civil War was a period of tremendous growth in business, commerce, industry. Agriculture was still king. But between the end of the Revolution and 1801, the states issued charters to some three hundred corporations. Most of these were infrastructure corporations: turnpikes, toll bridges, ferries, railroads; some were banks and insurance companies. Some were water supply companies. Transportation definitely came to dominate the business of chartering corporations. In Pennsylvania, there were 2,333 business corporations chartered by special act between 1790 and 1860; almost two thirds of them were transportation companies; the rest were in insurance and banking, gas and water companies; only 7.7 percent were manufacturing companies; but this was of course the wave of the future.

The corporation of the early nineteenth century was in many ways different from the corporation of today. Today, forming a corporation means very little more than filling out some forms and mailing a fee to the state capital. But at one time corporations were chartered one by one; each charter was a separate act of the legislature. Charters were custom-crafted. Not all of them had limited liability; not all of them gave perpetual life. They often contained quite precise specifications. For example, a charter to build a railroad might set out, in great detail, where the railroad would begin and end. The Georgia legislature, in 1857, issued a charter to the "Ocmulgee and Altamaha Steam Navigation Company," and "empowered" the company to carry passengers and freight "between the cities of Savannah and Macon, or on any of navigable waters in the State of Georgia, or between said city of Savannah and any Atlantic port."[9] The corporate charter of today is broad and sweeping; it basically authorizes the company to do whatever it wishes, whenever it wishes, in whatever business it wishes. A pizza parlor, incorporated, can decide to close the restaurant and open a shop selling Christmas tree decorations; or start a software business. But the Ocmulgee steamship company had to stick to exactly what the legislature specified; anything else would be "ultra vires," that is, beyond its powers. Any change would have to come from the legislature.

A NOTABLE INSTANCE: THE CASE OF THE CHARLES RIVER BRIDGE

In 1785, the state of Massachusetts issued a charter authorizing a group of businessmen in Cambridge, Massachusetts, to build a toll bridge over the Charles River. The bridge was built, and went into operation; in fact, it was enormously profitable. But in 1828, the Massachusetts legislature chartered another company to build another bridge, quite close to the toll bridge; *this* bridge was supposed to charge tolls for only six years; after that, the bridge would become a free bridge, and the property of the state. The owners of the Charles River Bridge, naturally, protested; the free bridge was bound to destroy the value of their investment. They brought a lawsuit to stop the bridge, and after a long journey, winding its way through the courts, the case ended up before the United States Supreme Court.[10]

There, too, it had a rather lengthy history. The case was first argued in March 1831. The Court was unable to agree; and ordered the case continued. A motion for reargument was accepted by the Court in 1833. In July 1835, Chief Justice John Marshall died; another justice also died, and still another resigned. The case was finally reargued and decided in 1837, under the new chief justice, Roger Brooke Taney. By this time, the second bridge had become a free bridge; and the old Charles River Bridge had become essentially worthless.

Chief Justice Taney wrote the main opinion, turning down the claims of the Charles River Bridge company.[11] There was also a dissent, written by Justice Joseph Story. Taney's opinion, in majestic and sweeping prose, rejected the arguments advanced by the owners of the Charles River Bridge. Their key point was this: essentially, by giving them the right to build the bridge, the legislature promised not to charter another bridge that would wipe out the value of their investment. No, said Taney, the first charter said nothing *explicitly* about any such promise; and he refused to read the promise into the charter. At the end of his opinion, he delivered himself of a long paean of praise to progress, science, modernity. Old ways, old franchises, had to give way to the new.

Story, for his part, argued that, indeed, a promise not to build a competing bridge was necessarily *implied* in the charter. Why would anybody invest in bridges or any other risky enterprise, under a charter, if the legislature could make the charter worthless? Interestingly, Taney and Story shared many values and assumptions. Both believed in progress, in fostering and encouraging enterprise. The dispute was over means, not ends. Once more we see that the sacredness of property has to be taken with a grain of salt. Once again, the new, progressive, dynamic property—the new bridge—trumped the rights of the old bridge. And attitudes toward "enterprise" were not the same as attitudes toward *corporations* or other entities that held franchises, which were in effect little monopolies. These, like the old bridge, were less favored than forward-looking enterprise.

The old bridge, with its bothersome tolls, stood in the way of progress. But opposition to *this* kind of monopoly is not the same as the opposition to the "trusts" and giant corporations of the later nineteenth century. The problem of the old bridge was not that it crushed the little guy, but that it stifled growth. This was the same charge leveled, for example, against land speculators. These speculators never, of course, intended to keep the land for themselves—they were not intent on building up great "estates." Their crime was that they kept land fallow, waiting for a higher market; and that they frustrated the passions of the settlers who pressed forward inexorably toward the west.

Technically, the Charles River Bridge case turned on the meaning of the so-called contracts clause of the Constitution. The federal Constitution provides that no state can pass any law "impairing the obligation of a contract." Exactly what this meant was not always clear; but at core, the clause was probably intended to make it impossible for states to interfere too much with the rights of creditors. The clause was extremely important in constitutional litigation in the first half of the nineteenth century; it was especially invoked when state governments, during the periodic downturns in the business cycle, the panics and crashes that plagued the economy, tried to help out people in debt. It was a clause about the relationship of government and the economy, particularly in times of great financial uncertainty. A number of crucial cases, in the United States Supreme Court, turned on whether or not states could pass insolvency laws, and of what sort; or about debtor relief laws of various types.[12]

Fletcher v. Peck (1810)[13] was a landmark case on the meaning of the contracts clause. In 1794, the Georgia legislature sold an enormous chunk of land (about 35 million acres) to a group of land companies, for a bargain price. The companies had smoothed the way for the deal by bribing almost every member of the Georgia legislature. In the next election, the rascals were thrown out, and a new set of legislators came into office; they promptly repudiated the deal. Meanwhile, not surprisingly, the land companies had resold millions of their ill-gotten acres, to buyers who were supposedly innocent. The Supreme Court held that the new Georgia legislature lacked the power to undo the land sale—despite the fraud. The grant of land, said the Court, amounted to a contract between the state and the grantees; and the legislature had no right to "impair" this contract. In *Dartmouth College v. Woodward* (1819)[14] the Supreme Court went a step further. Dartmouth College had been chartered in 1769. In 1816, the legislature passed laws that revised the charter, and changed the way the college was to be run. This was done for political reasons—mainly to get rid of the old trustees. The old trustees protested, on behalf of the college, and John Marshall's Supreme Court agreed with them. The original charter was a kind of "contract" between the state and the college, and later legislatures had no power to change it.

Not many people cared very much about the fate of this small college in New Hampshire. This was, on the surface, a strictly local affair. But Dartmouth College was a corporation—to be sure, a nonprofit corporation—and it had a charter. The logic of the case applied to all corporations, including banks and business corporations, since they all had charters from the state. The decision meant, then, that charters were sacred:

once granted, the state had no power to "impair" them. In practice, it proved rather easy to get around the Dartmouth College doctrine: legislatures simply inserted, into *new* charters, the right to alter or amend them; this right then became part of the "contract." Still, there was an important principle and issue in the case—it was, in a way, a sister issue to the issue in the Charles River Bridge case. The issue was how far the state could go in interfering with property rights; and how far it *should* go in guaranteeing a favorable climate for enterprise.

Thus, as we saw, the law in action reflected the general culture; and that general culture was a culture of enterprise, of growth, of progress. But where there is enterprise, there is also risk, where there is risk, there is failure; and failure was epidemic in the nineteenth century. There was, as we noted, no social safety net; yet there *was* a social demand, especially during hard times, for relief, for security, for help for those who faltered. The whole point of the "contracts clause" was to prevent states from going too far in helping out debtors. All states passed laws that protected at least *some* basic items from the clutch of creditors. During most of the century, there was no general bankruptcy law; but there were state insolvency laws, and schemes of one sort or another to save the victims of the volcanic eruptions of the business cycle.

The basic problem was both cultural and economic. There was a shortage of hard money in the country, no real banking system in the modern sense; yet the whole structure of enterprise floated on a sea of credit. Businesses sold on credit and bought on credit. Merchants borrowed money from banks, or from their suppliers; they sold to customers, who in turn owed them money to pay for what they bought. When one link in the chain began to weaken, there was trouble up and down the line. When the customer failed to pay, the merchant was hard-pressed to pay his suppliers; and this squeezed them as well. Credit problems were the economic side of the problem. But the need for credit was so very great because of a culture of risk-taking and optimism; a culture that encouraged men (and mostly men) to go into business, to be their own bosses, so that thousands of "farmboys, clerks, and young mechanics" leaped impetuously "into the commercial fray on their own financial responsibility."[15] A few of these entrepreneurs struck it rich; most either barely survived—or sank underneath a load of debt. It was also a culture of second chances. Imprisonment for debt was abolished. In its place came laws that wiped the slate clean, and let a failed businessman start over, if he could.

NOTES

1. William J. Novak, *The People's Welfare: Law and Regulation in Nineteenth-Century America* (1996), pp. 198–200.

2. 9 Stat. 519 (act of Sept. 28, 1850).

3. Benjamin Horace Hibbard, *A History of the Public Land Policies* (1965), p. 275.

4. 9 Stat. 520 (act of Sept. 28, 1850).

5. Gene Eric Salecker, *Disaster on the Mississippi: The Sultana Explosion, April 27, 1865* (1996).

6. 45 Mass. (4 Metc.) 49 (1842).

7. The English case, quite famous, was *Priestley v. Fowler,* 3 M. & W. 1 (Ex. 1837); the South Carolina case was *Murray v. South Carolina Railroad,* 36 So. Car. L. (1 McMul.) 385 (1841).

8. The phrase, as we noted before, comes from James Willard Hurst, *Law and the Conditions of Freedom in the Nineteenth-Century United States* (1956), especially chapter one, "The Release of Energy."

9. Laws Ga. 1857, pp. 81–82.

10. The case is discussed in Stanley I. Kutler, *Privilege and Creative Destruction: The Charles River Bridge Case* (1971).

11. *Proprietors of the Charles River Bridge v. Proprietors of the Warren Bridge,* 11 Pet. 420 (1837).

12. *Sturges v. Crowninshield,* 4 Wheat. (17 U.S.) 122 (1819); *Ogden v. Saunders,* 12 Wheat. (25 U.S.) 213 (1827).

13. 6 Cranch (10 U.S.) 87 (1810).

14. 4 Wheat. (17 U.S.) 518 (1819).

15. Edward J. Balleisen, *Navigating Failure: Bankruptcy and Commercial Society in Antebellum America* (2001), p. 50.

FOUR

FAMILY, RACE, AND THE LAW

Family law is the law of marriage, divorce, marital property, adoption, and related matters. Like everything else in the law, it reflects what is happening in society, and what is happening in society has a profound impact on family life and family relations. Family law was completely revamped in the nineteenth century—the enormous changes in society left their mark on this field as well as all others.

What was family law like at the beginning of the nineteenth century? It would be only a slight exaggeration to say that it gave everything to the father, legally speaking, and very little to anybody else in the family. In 1800, for example, if a woman owned a piece of land—land she inherited, for example—when she married, she lost title to the land; it passed into the hands of her husband. Husband and wife were, as the saying went, one flesh; but the husband was very definitely in charge of that flesh. And more than the flesh. The wife had, in many ways, as few rights as a newborn baby or a lunatic. A married woman could not buy or sell without her husband's permission, she could not leave property behind in her will, she could not raise money by mortgaging her land. And if the marriage ended in separation or divorce, the law gave the father, not the mother, the right to custody of the children, except in rare cases.

All this changed drastically during the nineteenth century. Married women's property laws gave married women the right to own land, to buy and sell, to enter into contracts and make wills. These laws were passed in bits and pieces, and from state to state, from about the middle of the century; by the end of the century, they were fairly complete and fairly universal. The custody rule also changed. Custody did not automatically go to the father any longer. It followed the "best interests of the child," and (for children of "tender years") that usually meant the mother, not the father.

In the nineteenth century, too, for the first time, the law recognized the formal, legal *adoption* of children. There was no such concept in the common law. A child was a blood child or nothing. The first legal adoptions came in the form of "private acts," passed one by one in the various states. Some of these statutes explicitly referred to adoption: thus a Mississippi statute of 1844 recited that one Aaron Wickliffe had "adopted" his niece Mary Worthington; the statute changed her name to Mary Wickliffe, gave her "all the rights of a child of his blood," and made her "capable in law of inheriting" his property, just as if she were "the issue of his body";[1] Massachusetts, in 1851, was the first state to pass a general adoption statute. It set up a procedure for adoption in court (rather than through petitioning the legislature), and laid down the rule that the adopted child had full inheritance rights. The Massachusetts statute was widely copied by other states.

The actual text of the Massachusetts law, and even the private adoption acts, make it quite plain that these were statutes about *inheritance*. Nobody needs an adoption law to take in a child, love it, care for it. In a time when many women died in childbirth, and both men and women often died early, thousands of children were raised by aunts, grandparents, and other relatives. But to give the child inheritance rights, in a society where middle-class people owned land (a farm, a lot in town) and had a stake in society—this took something more formal and legal, something more than a home and a hug. The same feature might explain another peculiarity of American law in the nineteenth century: the common law marriage. This is a much misunderstood term. A common law marriage—where it is recognized—is an absolutely valid marriage. Most states in the nineteenth century recognized the common law marriage—a marriage entered into by agreement, without any formalities whatsoever. If a man and woman in one of these states, sitting in front of a roaring fire and feeling a burst of love, simply decided to be husband and wife, and said so, then from that moment on they *were* legally husband and wife—without a license, a preacher, witnesses, or anything beyond their naked promise.

There was no such thing as common law marriage in England. Whatever the roots of the common law marriage, it was extremely useful in a society with poor record-keeping, but widespread ownership of land. Suppose both husband and wife were dead, and the question was: who gets the family farm? If we *presume* a common law marriage, even if nobody can prove a ceremonial marriage, then the children are legitimate children, not bastards; and they inherit the land. What the rule meant in practice was this: when two people lived together, as husband and wife, in attitudes of full bourgeois respectability, they were assumed to be married, one way or another, even if no records of any marriage could be found. Here, too, as in the rise of adoption, what made such a rule useful was the widespread ownership of land.

Divorce has had a complex history in the United States. Everybody knows that Henry VIII divorced his first wife, and that this touched off his separation from the Church of Rome; but it is much less well known that divorce was not available for ordinary folks at all in England, until 1857. The only way to get a divorce was through an Act of Parliament—which meant, in effect, that only nobles and the very wealthy had any chance at divorce. In some southern states, this was also the case: only the state legislature could grant a divorce. A law of Florida Territory, in 1844, recited that one Duglas Dummett had "abandoned his wife Frances . . . and . . . wholly failed to provide means of support for her and her child"; Frances had "petitioned" to be divorced, and the law duly decreed that the "marriage contract" between the two was "dissolved and annulled and the said parties are hereby absolutely divorced from the bonds of matrimony."[2] In the northern states—and later also in the south—the law allowed the so-called judicial divorce. To get a divorce, either husband or wife would file a lawsuit, complaining that the other partner had committed some act that was "grounds" for divorce. Each state had its own list of such grounds. These were different from state to state, but typically included adultery, desertion, and often cruelty. In New Hampshire, joining the Shakers (who rejected sex) was grounds for divorce. In Tennessee, a woman who was pregnant by another man, at the time of marriage, was entitled to a divorce. Some states were strict, some were lax. New York was strict: it allowed divorce, essentially, only for adultery. South Carolina did not allow divorce at all.

Divorce was always controversial. It was forbidden to Roman Catholics. Protestants allowed it, but basically disapproved of it. Yet the demand for divorce rose steadily. Family structure was changing; but perhaps even more important was the economic structure. Millions of ordinary men and families had a farm, or some other piece of property. This meant that millions of people were in the market for legal devices to legitimate and regularize their family relationships—for purposes of inheritance, very notably. A man, or woman, who wanted to get rid of an old family, and start a new one, needed a divorce—otherwise the new children would be illegitimate, the new "wife" a mistress, and the rights to the property would remain with the old nuclear family. This was certainly a factor underlying the demand for divorce. Still, despite the demand, divorce reform never had smooth sailing. Adoption laws spread easily from state to state; but the demand for divorce bumped up against powerful religious and moral objections. As a result, divorce laws were sticky, tough, resistant to change.

What developed was what we might call a dual system.[3] On the surface, strict laws remained on the books. Divorce was available only to innocent victims of bad husbands or wives. Consensual divorce—divorce by mutual agreement—was legally impossible, in every state. "Collusion"—an agreement between husband and wife to get a divorce—was forbidden, according to law. The mere fact that both parties felt it was time to say goodbye had no legal effect, unless there were "grounds." In practice, the situation was entirely different. In fact, after 1870, the vast majority of divorces *were* collusive, and the court proceedings were a mere charade or worse. Of course, "agreement" does not mean that both husband and wife were eager to get a divorce. It only means that the two had decided not to fight out the matter in court.

Collusion took different forms in different states. Since New York essentially allowed divorce only for adultery, a number of exotic practices developed. The most scandalous was a scheme we might call soft-core adultery. The husband registered at a hotel. In his room, he would get partially un-dressed. A woman would arrive. She, too, would take off most of her clothes. A photographer appeared, took their picture sitting on the bed together; the woman got dressed, pocketed her fee, and left. The photographs would be presented to court as evidence of adultery. One gets something of the fla-vor of the system from the title of an article in the *New York Sunday Mirror,* from 1934: "I Was the Unknown Blonde in 100 New York Divorces."[4] In other states, the "cruelty" was a sham: the wife would allege that he had slapped her twice, or humiliated her, or otherwise made her life miserable. The husband would file no answer, no defense; and divorce would be granted by default.

Collusion was only one of several ways around the strict divorce laws. Another was to travel to a state that made divorce easier to get—the so-called divorce mills. These rose and fell in the nineteenth century, as a number of states tried to cash in on the business of migratory divorces: Indiana, then North and South Dakota. The divorce mills had short "residency" periods—a woman (or man) who wanted a divorce would travel to (say) South Dakota, spend a few weeks there, then file for divorce. Other states, in general, had to recognize these divorces as valid.[5] The divorce mills tended to be unstable—they were denounced as immoral by clergy and moral leaders, who then pressed for tighter rules. The most recent (and most permanent) was Nevada, which in the twentieth century also legalized gambling and prostitution; it made itself a marriage mill as well as a divorce mill. Nevada was a barren desert state with a tiny population and not much of an economic base. Moral scruples seemed to be in short supply in Nevada. Indeed, it built its economy on the basis of its laxity and sovereignty: essentially, Nevada got rich making legal what was forbidden in neighboring California.

It is interesting that a system built on lies and detours should survive for something on the order of a century. Judges were perfectly aware of what was going on in the world of divorce. A few judges complained or cracked down once in a while; but mostly they turned a blind eye. Like all dual systems, divorce law rested on a compromise. The official law remained more or less as it was; and perhaps it was something at least of a minor deterrence. It certainly made divorce more troublesome and expensive. But the unofficial law allowed people to get their divorces, despite the official law. Obviously nobody was satisfied with the system—or with any of the other dual systems in the law. And there were many of these—laws against prostitution, for example, which were unenforced in the "red-light districts." Nobody actively *wants* dual systems; but they persist because they are rough, unlovable compromises—or, if you will, stalemates—between a moral high ground and what people actually want or do.

In the first half of the twentieth century, there were definite signs of decay in the dual system of divorce. The grounds became broader in some states—in Wyoming, a spouse could get a divorce for "indignities" that made the marriage "intolerable," a very loose category.[6] One or two states even began to allow divorce on grounds of "incompatibility," which meant, really, allowing consensual divorce. By the 1950s, quite a few states permitted divorce without any "grounds" at all, provided the couple had been living apart for a certain number of years.

In 1970, California passed the first "no-fault" divorce statute. No longer did the parties have to allege any "grounds" for divorce. The whole dirty apparatus of collusion was swept away. The only question for the court was whether the marriage had "irretrievably" broken down. And in practice, this requirement soon disappeared. Now the sole question was, did somebody—either husband or wife—want to end the relationship? If the answer was yes, the divorce was automatically granted. This went way beyond consensual divorce. It was not divorce by agreement: it was divorce at the option of either husband or wife.

The no-fault idea began in California, but it soon spread, in one form or another, to most of the other states. No-fault is today the norm, not the exception. Divorce rates continue to be very high. Many people take a high divorce rate to be a sign of the decay of marriage, and the end of the family as we traditionally knew it. There is, of course, something to this. But, paradoxically, the high divorce rate is also testimony to the enduring popularity of marriage—indeed, as William O'Neill has pointed out, in his study of divorce in the Progressive period, divorce rates rise because of the heightened meaning of marriage.[7] Traditional marriages do not put enormous demands on the spouses: they have separate roles, separate spheres, and their marital "duties" are limited. Companionate marriage raises the stakes. Now man and wife are supposed to be equals: to share their lives as lovers, best friends, and co-partners. In practice, of course, thousands of marriages fall far short of this goal. In the first place, patriarchy is still alive and well; and there is a long gap between the theory of equality and the practice. Millions of men and women still accept or require this division of labor. Still, even in more or less "traditional" marriages, men and women have been demanding more and more out of each other. If the marriage sputtered and failed, emotionally, sexually, or in any other way, they wanted out—and the chance to start over again. And divorce was and is the gateway to remarriage.

No-fault divorce suggests yet another turn of the wheel—something even beyond companionate marriage. It suggests a view of marriage less as a working partnership than as something intensely *personal,* a mode of self-realization; a profoundly individual choice, and one that has to be undone if it fails to satisfy or bring about its goal for either of the partners. In any event, no-fault divorce means that divorce itself is no longer a legal issue. A couple without children, and not much or any property to speak of, can dissolve their marriage quickly and cheaply—and even if only one of them wants out. But no-fault divorce did not put family lawyers out of business—quite the contrary. Family law remains complex and entangled. Questions of property and child custody probably come up more frequently than ever; and may be even more difficult than before. For one thing, a significant number of men are now demanding custody—and sometimes getting it. The divorce rate is still high—shockingly high. But this is only to be expected in an age that puts so much stress on individual fulfillment and personal growth.

Divorce is a legal institution. There have been societies without divorce—and there is still no such thing as a legal divorce in Chile. Only somebody impossibly naive would jump to the conclusion that everybody in Chile is happily married and committed for life. Divorce does not *cause* families to break up. But many people have been and are convinced that without easy divorce there would be fewer "broken homes." These people have nothing in the way of evidence to back them up. But in American politics, gut feelings almost always trump science. Louisiana, in 1997, introduced a new wrinkle into family law.[8] Bride and groom can now choose between two forms of marriage. There is ordinary marriage; and there is also "covenant marriage." The parties to a "covenant marriage" agree that marriage "is a lifelong arrangement." They give up their right to a no-fault divorce. In fact, "covenant marriage," despite the rhetoric, is not really a life sentence. The partners *can* get a divorce; but only if there are traditional "grounds" for it (adultery, desertion, and the like). So far, not too many couples have signed up for covenant marriage. But the idea has caught on in a few other states—Arizona, for example.[9] Whether "covenant marriage" has much of a future, or is likely to make much of a difference, seems dubious.

Marriages in contemporary America break up at a very high rate; but marriage remains a strong institution. It has, however, a powerful competitor: cohabitation. Millions of people now live together in a relationship that used to be called "living in sin." Sin has almost completely dropped out of the picture—at least for most people, especially in the urban centers. What was once an object of gossip and scandal hardly raises an eyebrow in the early twenty-first century.

Cohabitation has spawned its own package of legal problems; and like all social developments, sooner or later it had to have its day in court. The defendant in the famous California case of *Marvin v. Marvin* (1976)[10] was a movie star, Lee Marvin. The plaintiff was a woman he lived with for many years, Michele Triola Marvin. They were never married. When they split up, she sued him, claiming he had promised her a share of his earnings if she gave up her own career and came to live with him as his housemate and companion. Lee Marvin had a simple but (he thought) powerful defense. Legally, Michele could not enforce a contract that called for a "meretricious relationship," the rather smarmy legal term for a long-term sexual affair. And indeed there was a raft of older cases that said exactly that.

But the California Supreme Court brushed these cases aside. The court did make a halfhearted attempt to explain them away; but the heart of the decision was the court's admission that the "mores of ... society have ... changed ... radically in regard to cohabitation." The court "cannot impose a standard based on alleged moral considerations that have apparently been so widely abandoned by so many." The lower court had therefore been wrong in throwing the case out.

The actual result of the case, in the end, was something of an anticlimax. The California Supreme Court had sent the case back down to the trial court, and ordered the court to hold a trial on the issue. At the trial, Michele essentially ended up losing her case. But the principle of the case caused quite a stir; it made headlines, and spawned hundreds of jokes, cartoons, editorial comments—and prophecies of doom. It would lead to blackmail, it would lead to a staggering number of lawsuits, it would ruin relationships, and so on. Some states followed the lead of the *Marvin* case; some did not, or limited it drastically. Probably very few cohabitors bring a *Marvin*-type lawsuit, in any given year. The case *is* a landmark, however. It is one more sign of the death of an age dominated by a particular culture: the Protestant white culture, firmly based on a code of traditional morality.

THE SKELETON IN AMERICA'S CLOSET: RACE RELATIONS IN THE NINETEENTH CENTURY

The "peculiar institution," slavery, not only persisted after independence; it grew stronger in the nineteenth century. Hundreds of thousands of black slaves worked in the cotton fields, on large plantations; or as house servants; and in every conceivable job, in the southern states. In the first half of the nineteenth century, slavery also became a *political* issue; and a hotly contested one. Slavery had existed in every colony; but the northern states abolished slavery after the Revolution; and by the early nineteenth century, there was a clear divide between slave states and free states, which had not been the case before. And there was a strong abolitionist movement in the north—which also had not been the case in the past. Meanwhile, the southern states continued, and expanded, their harsh codes of law about slaves and slavery. Slaves could not legally marry; it was a crime to teach a slave to read and write; they were subject, as before, to the almost absolute will of the owner.

No doubt there were masters who dealt kindly with their slaves; others were almost unspeakably cruel. On most plantations, the whip was liberally used to keep slaves in line. It was an open secret that many southern whites had slave mistresses; some masters set these women and their children free, or openly acknowledged them, but this was exceptional. There were also free blacks in the south—emancipated slaves and their descendants; but they were everywhere treated as second-class citizens or worse. They had no role whatever in the political system.

Slaves were vital to the southern economy; and, more and more, to the southern way of life. Slavery was more than a labor system; it was also a caste system, an essential aspect of social structure in such states as Alabama or Texas. The north was committed to a free labor system. The fissure between north and south grew wider, and, although it was papered over with political compromises in the first half of the century, eventually the country cracked in two, during the great Civil War, mostly along the great fault line of slavery.[11] This was a war to preserve the Union—but it was slavery that had split the Union; and the war also became, in the end, a crusade against slavery. The north won the war, and slavery lost. Lincoln issued his emancipation proclamation, and, after the war, the Thirteenth Amendment to the Constitution put the final nail in the coffin of the system of slavery.

Or so it seemed. The north had, quite genuinely, despised slavery as an institution. But it did not, by any means, accept the idea of racial equality. Racism was at its most virulent and intransigent in the states of the old Confederacy; but nowhere—not in Chicago, or Boston, or any other northern bastion of "free labor"—did white people in general accept black people as brothers or equals or co-voyagers on the journey through life. Hence, after a brief interlude, the south relapsed into white supremacy; and the north into malign indifference. During the Reconstruction period, there were black officeholders, blacks in Congress, blacks on the bench, blacks in state legislatures. But by the end of the century, white supremacy was in the saddle everywhere in the south. Blacks were driven out of office, terrorized, stripped of the right to vote by one legal and illegal stratagem or another. Segregation became the norm, and the United States Supreme Court, in *Plessy v. Ferguson* (1896),[12] gave segregation its seal of approval: so long as institutions were separate but equal, they were constitutionally acceptable. The south rigorously enforced the "separate" part of this equation; the "equal" part was simply a sham.

The blacks were no longer slaves; but most of them were little better than serfs. Most of them were farmworkers, tied to the land by sharecropping contracts, or through a network of laws that kept them in place—for example, vagrancy laws, which punished unemployment, and laws against "entice-ment," which in effect made it a crime to offer a black worker a better job. The American south had become a caste system, in which all whites outranked all blacks; a system in which a black man or woman had virtually no chance of fulfilling what for whites would be the normal American ambitions and dreams.

Race was also an element in the scandalous treatment of the Chinese, who were concentrated on the west coast. The Chinese exclusion laws prevented the Chinese from immigrating, or from becoming citizens once they were here. Asians were barred from owning land in California and other states. Under the so-called gentlemen's agreement of 1907–1908, between the United States and Japan, the Japa-nese government agreed to stop Japanese workers from emigrating to the United States. West coast states also prohib-ited marriages between whites and people with "Mongolian blood." The United States Supreme Court, in one case, faced the issue of whether a "high-class Hindu" had the right to be-come a citizen. The answer was no. There was a clear "racial difference" between this "high-class Hindu" and the rest of the population; and "assimilation" was out of the question.

For blacks, the "solution" to the "problem" was subjugation and a caste system; for Asians, the solution was exclusion. For Native Americans, the "solution" was more complex. It was, at first, conquest in war; then settlers and the government stole their land, killing many and herding the survivors onto "reservations." But when the tribes were no longer a military threat, and the best land had already been taken, the national goal became assimilation. The Dawes Act of 1887 tried to destroy the traditional land tenure systems of the native peoples. The idea was to turn the Indians into family farmers. The result was, however, disastrous: wholesale fraud and chicanery, and, at the end of the process, the natives had lost hundreds of thousands of acres of land. Taboos against intermarriage with Native Americans were never as strong as they were in black-white relations. The policy goal was to wean the tribes away from their religion, language, and culture, and turn them into regular Americans. There were no doubt many who believed this was in the best interests of the members of the tribe. Here, too, the road to hell—and to cultural genocide—can be paved with the best of intentions.

NOTES

1. Laws Miss. 1844, ch. 144, pp. 329–30.

2. Laws Terr. Fla. 1844, p. 67.

3. On the divorce system in this period, see Lawrence M. Friedman, "A Dead Language: Divorce Law and Practice Before No-Fault," *Virginia Law Review* 86:1497 (2000).

4. *New York Sunday Mirror*, Feb. 25, 1934 (magazine section).

5. This was because the Constitution requires states to give "full faith and credit" to the "judicial proceedings" of other states (Article IV, Section 1). Despite this, at least some migratory divorces were under a legal cloud.

6. Wyo. Stats. 1899, sec. 2988.

7. William L. O'Neill, *Divorce in the Progressive Era* (1967).

8. La. Rev. Stat. Ann. sec. 272 (2000).

9. Ariz. Laws 1998, ch. 135.

10. 18 Cal. 3rd 660, 557 P. 2d 106, 134 Cal. R. 815 (1976).

11. There were slave states that did not secede: Kentucky, Missouri, Maryland.

12. 163 U.S. 537 (1896).

FIVE

CRIME AND PUNISHMENT IN THE REPUBLIC

Every society has a list, formal or informal, of behaviors that are forbidden, and every society tries to punish or control people who violate these norms. Crimes are behaviors that the state undertakes to punish. Each society has its own list of crimes. It is hard to imagine a society without *some* kind of rule against unlawful killing, or against some form of stealing. But even these classic crimes are defined by each society in its own particular way. The catalogue of crimes, in other words, depends very much on culture, time, and place.

In the colonial period, fornication (for example) was one of the most commonly punished crimes—unmarried people having sex with each other. Blasphemy, idleness, Sabbath-breaking, and skipping church services were also crimes in such colonies as Massachusetts Bay. Not one of these is a crime in, say, modern California. Colonial society took seriously, and punished, matters that would be considered quite private today. So, in 1656, in Springfield, Massachusetts, one Obadiah Miller complained that his wife abused him "with reproachfull tearmes or names as calling him foole toad and vermine"; she also scratched him and threatened to "knock him on the head." (She also said she did not love him.) For this "vile misbehaviour toward her husband," the local court ordered her to be whipped with "stripes" on her "naked body"; she avoided this fate by humbling herself and making "earnest protestations" that she would act more nicely toward Obadiah.[1]

There was little or no concept of what we now call "victimless" crime in the colonial period. If two grown-ups want to gamble, or have sex, this would be defined today as a "victimless" crime—if a crime at all, since nobody forced anybody else to do something against his will. Whether the rest of us approve or not of the sex, or the gambling, or the drinking, is now considered (by many people) to be totally irrelevant. Society, then, should only punish crimes with victims: people who were wronged, against their will. Of course, consistency is never to be found in human affairs: many people who accept drinking or gambling or nonmarital sex are only too eager to punish a man who sells cocaine to a very willing buyer.

The colonials, particularly in Massachusetts Bay and other Puritan colonies, had no concept of the "victimless" crime. All evil acts were crimes, consensual or not. God would surely pass judgment on a sinful society. Fornication, in other words, was not truly victimless: when these two people rolled in consensual hay, they were threatening the whole community; they were bringing down God's wrath on themselves and their neighbors.

The colonists, particularly in the Puritan colonies, regularly punished violations of the moral code. They made no real distinction between sin and crime. The records are replete with punishments for fornication, idleness, Sabbath-breaking, and the like. Fornication, indeed, was, as we said, very frequently punished. Mostly, this was a crime committed by servants. They were punished with fines, sometimes with a whipping; occasionally, the court ordered a couple to get married. These were small, tight-knit communities—it was (relatively) easy to find a fornicator out, since there were so few places to hide, and so much snooping and gossip. What is more, there was community consensus, apparently, about the norms in question: the idea that fornication was wrong and ought to be punished. These are two conditions that underlay the colonial system of criminal justice: a small community; and moral consensus. They are utterly lacking today. A person walking in a San Francisco park, in 2001, who thought he saw two people having sex in the bushes, would either stare at them, take a picture, or (probably) go on walking. Big-city life is impersonal, complex, and morally heterogeneous.

Sins were not confined to sins of the flesh. There were also sins against religion. Many colonists had come to the New World to get away from religious persecution, but they believed that theirs was the one true religion, which gave them the right to persecute everybody else. Under the laws of Massachusetts Bay, for example, Jesuits were not allowed on the sacred soil of Massachusetts; all Jesuits were to be banished; the punishment for a second offense was (in theory) death. An exception was made for a Jesuit "cast upon our shoars, by shipwrack or other accident," but even this unfortunate was to stay only until he had "opportunitie of passage for his departure." Heresy was also a crime; and heretics were to be sentenced to "Banishment."

Nowadays, we take it for granted that the main way of punishing criminals is to clap them into some sort of prison. But this was, in fact, not the general rule before well into the nineteenth century. There were colonial jails, but they were mostly used for debtors, and for people waiting to be tried for their crimes. Jails were ramshackle affairs, not the "big house" of the nineteenth century. A small society, bent on returning offenders to the community, making heavy use of shame and stigma to punish crime—and with a severe shortage of labor—was not a society likely to imprison its herd of black sheep.

Punishment, then, almost never meant loss of freedom. Punishment was money (fines), physical pain (whipping), shaming (sitting in the stocks, for example), or in extreme cases banishment or death. The main idea was to hold the wrongdoer up to public obloquy. The *community* played an important role in criminal justice. Public degradation would force wrongdoers to see the error of their ways, and help to integrate them back into the community—a basic goal of the system. This is why punishment was always in the open, and before a crowd; and why the colonists relied so heavily on ways of punishing that tried to shame the miscreants— making them sit in the stocks, dunking their heads in pails of water, and the like. The idea was to teach a lesson—to the person who committed the offense; and also to the community, which watched and saw what was going on. Hanging was itself a public spectacle. It, too, was done in public; and before large crowds. Often, the condemned man made a speech from the gallows—confessing his crimes, warning people not to follow in his footsteps, and expressing some sort of hope for salvation. Thus hanging, too, was a kind of theatrical event— a form of didactic drama.

Under an early Massachusetts statute on burglary and theft, in the 1660s, a first offender was to be "branded on the forehead with the letter (B)"; a criminal who repeated was to receive another branding and a sound whipping as well; and anyone who committed a third offense was to be "put to death, as being incorrigible."[2] Note that the punishments were bodily; and that they left visible marks behind; note, too, that death was reserved as punishment for hopeless cases. Branding with a hot iron was indeed a common punishment; a burglar in Connecticut in 1773, for example, was branded on the forehead with a capital B; one of his ears was cut off as additional punishment.[3] The famous "scarlet letter" for adultery is another example of the habit of publicly marking and identifying wrongdoers. In Richmond, Virginia, in 1729, a black slave, Tony, was accused of perjury; the sheriff was ordered to "Naile one of his Ears to the pillory and there to stand for . . . one hour and then cutt the said Ear off"; after another hour, the slave was to lose the other ear. In addition, he received thirty-nine lashes.[4] In North Carolina, castration was sometimes used as a punishment for slaves.[5]

The colonists realized that not everybody would or could

respond to punishment; that some people were incorrigible. These were the people who had to be banished, or put to death: repeat offenders, for example. Witches were certainly in this category—if a woman has sold her soul to the devil, she is lost forever. There is no way to bring her back to society; society must feel free to get rid of her.

All of the colonies recognized, and made use of, the death penalty, which meant, in practice, the hangman. Occasionally, other methods were tried—a woman was burned to death in Pennsylvania in 1731 for murdering her husband—but this was unusual. There were fewer capital crimes in the colonies than in England; and the colonists seemed to use the death penalty rather less. In England, if you stole goods worth more than a certain amount, you could be hanged for it; in the colonies, property crimes led to the death penalty only for repeat offenders. A study of colonial Pennsylvania[6] found 141 convictions in capital cases up until the Revolution—almost a century; of these, 41 were pardoned, 26 reprieved. The actual number executed seems to have been 74, or less than one a year. The Pennsylvania figures did not include the deaths of black slaves, who were handled separately; but there were not that many slaves in Pennsylvania, and probably very few were executed. The situation was, of course, quite different in the southern colonies. There capital punishment was much more frequent; many of the condemned were slaves, but even if we drop them out of the picture, the south remains bloodier than the north.

Capital punishment was not frequent in Massachusetts Bay. There were, apparently, only fifteen executions before 1660 (the population, to be sure, was small)—four for murder, two for infanticide, three for sexual offenses, two for witchcraft. Four Quakers were put to death. There were fifty-six executions between 1630 and 1692. During the famous Salem witchcraft trials, in the 1690s, nineteen people were executed, two died in prison, and one man, Giles Corey, was pressed to death under rocks because he refused to plead or to testify.[7]

Much of the colonial system seems exceedingly strange to us today. Massachusetts punished crimes we no longer punish, and some (witchcraft) that we believe were always figments of somebody's imagination. The system was in part less technical than ours, in part full of technicalities we have lost; it was also much less dominated by lawyers than the modern system. But other aspects of criminal justice would seem fairly familiar to a contemporary. Despite some zigs and zags, the system of trial by jury was in full use in the colonies. Many colonial institutions—grand jury indictment and oral examination of witnesses, for example—are still with us today. Criminal justice, thus, is a story of both continuity and change.

CRIME AND PUNISHMENT IN THE NINETEENTH CENTURY

After the war of independence, and especially during the nineteenth century, there were significant innovations in the system of criminal justice. Two particularly crucial innovations were the rise of the penitentiary and the development of urban police forces.

As we noted, the colonial criminal was whipped, fined, branded, banished, even hanged; but not imprisoned. The colonial theory of crime put heavy emphasis on community punishment. The system seemed to work, more or less, in small, tight, hierarchical communities. But by the time of the Revolution, the social underpinnings of the system were decaying. The population was growing fast. The cities were also growing; and they were filling up with a population much different from New England's godly communities: rowdy, bawdy, tumultuous. Riots and disorders were common. This situation gave rise both to the penitentiary and to the police system.

In a big city, decent people felt, quite naturally, that the general community—the public, the mob—was no longer a respectful, helpful auxiliary to criminal justice and its processes. The community was no longer a cure for deviance, but if anything the cause. Out of this idea came the penitentiary. The penitentiary was designed to remove the criminal from society, subject him to iron discipline, and radically change his habits and his frame of mind. In the postrevolutionary period, too, the states (especially in the north) cut down on the use of capital punishment. To a certain extent, the penitentiary was a substitute for the hangman.

The classic penitentiary—Cherry Hill in Pennsylvania (1829) is an excellent example—was radically different from the jerry-built jails of the colonial period. Cherry Hill was a massive, solemn building, surrounded by high walls, imposing, impregnable. Prisoners were locked up one to a cell; the cells were arranged in blocks, radiating out of a central core. Guards with guns manned the walls. Prisoners were utterly alone, and the prison was utterly silent. Prisoners were forbidden to speak. Regimentation and discipline were key aspects of prison life. The prisoners wore uniforms. Their hair was cut short. All prisoners in the great penitentiaries dressed alike, ate at the same time, moved in lockstep, went to bed at the same time. In some prisons, the prisoners labored in their cells; in others, they worked outside the cells, but always in silence. They followed the same dull, dreary routine, day in and day out. Letters were censored. Visits were restricted. This radical disjuncture, this severing of bonds with the outside world, was the key—it was believed—to rehabilitation.

The penitentiary would remake the man, and after taking this radical medicine he would be ready to go out again into the world.

After the Revolution, and especially in the early nineteenth century, considerable effort went into making the system more rational. The criminal law of the various states was reduced to a "code"; and whatever was not in the code could no longer be considered a crime. This meant the end of the doctrine of the common law crime. A common law crime was one that was not expressed in any formal law—not the subject of legislation. It was, in short, judge-made—like the rules of tort and contract. But criminal justice was considered different—and more dangerous. It was one thing for judges to bend and mold rules about broken bones, or agreements to sell a horse; quite another to give judges the power to send men to prison or to their deaths for something not clearly expressed in formal law. The revolutionary generation reacted against its image of the British system of justice—a system too arbitrary, too hierarchical for the more republican tastes of Americans.

CORRECTIONS AND ENFORCEMENT

Up until the nineteenth century, the "police" of cities and towns consisted of a motley crew of constables and night watchmen—a rather loose and inefficient system. Respectable people considered this totally inadequate in an age of urban violence. London established a metropolitan police force in 1829; and this was a model for the United States. New York was a pioneer in adopting a police force; but other cities were not far behind—Boston, Philadelphia, then, in the 1850s, such cities as New Orleans, Chicago, and Cincinnati. By the late nineteenth century, most American cities had police forces. And the police wore uniforms and badges: they were a kind of paramilitary force, on duty twenty-four hours a day.

Unfortunately, the parallel to a spit-and-polish, tightly disciplined army pretty much ended with the uniform and badge. There was a certain amount of movement toward professionalizing the police; but in most cities, men got on the police force through pull or clout; and the police were hardly models of decorum and legality. Corruption and brutality were rampant. This was particularly the case in the late nineteenth century.

The classic penitentiary, too, underwent dramatic change later in the century. The purity and rigor of the early days did not last long. The silent system was soon given up; it depended on keeping prisoners locked up one to a cell, but this was an expensive proposition. The penitentiary had relied on strict discipline and absolute regimentation. All prisoners were treated the same. Now penologists were anxious to make distinctions between types of prisoners. The penitentiary was replaced, in part, by "reformatories," which were less harsh and forbidding than the classic penitentiary, more geared toward rehabilitation. Elmira, in New York, opened in 1876, was an early example of the reformatory. Elmira was for young offenders (though not necessarily juveniles). Reformatories graded and classified prisoners, gave them good (or bad) marks for conduct, rewarded the good and held back the bad. In Massachusetts, in the 1920s, for example, prisoners earned "credits" for good conduct; a good record earned you a uniform with yellow chevrons, a bad record got you a uniform of "flaming, cardinal red"; and much less chance at early release.[8]

Prison officials and penologists, in the late nineteenth century, asked a familiar question: how can we separate out those prisoners who can be reformed, redeemed, returned to society; and those who cannot? One solution was the so-called indeterminate sentence. The idea was simple: when a man was convicted of a crime, the judge would not impose a definite sentence. Rather, the man would be sent to prison for some minimum term—usually a year. At the end of this term, the prison officials, who had had the chance to watch the prisoner, and see how he behaved, would decide on his long-term fate. The first general statute on the indeterminate sentence was adopted in New York, in 1889. Many other states followed by the early twentieth century.

There were other innovations along the same lines. One was the allowance of "good time"—credit—for good behavior, which could be used to shorten the term of imprisonment. Another was parole. Parole was a system of letting prisoners out of prison early, but subject to certain conditions, and (in theory at least) to supervision. There were some earlier examples, but parole caught on only after 1870. Twenty-five states had laws allowing parole by 1898.

Under an indeterminate sentence law, or a parole law, if two men broke into a store together, were caught, tried, and convicted, it was quite possible for them to spend very different amounts of time in prison for the exact same criminal act. One man might be locked up for a year or two, the other ten years or even longer. But this was not considered a defect in the system; quite the contrary. The whole point of these devices was to shift emphasis away from the offense, and put the emphasis on the offender himself—his character, his personality, his propensities for evil or for good. Of course, the shift was only relative: it still mattered, and very greatly, whether the crime was forging a check or cold-blooded murder.

Another reform, to the same general end, was probation—both for children and adults. Adult probation entered the law in California in 1903. Under a probation system, a person convicted of crime is spared prison altogether in exchange for a certain period of supervision by a probation officer. It is, in other words, a kind of pre-parole. This greatly humanized criminal justice—it spared thousands of men and women the terrors and tortures of prison—but it also shifted power to the probation officer; it injected yet another fairly arbitrary element into the system. Probation went mostly to first offenders, and to men or women who pleaded guilty. Even so, the defendant's fate rode on the probation report—and the report often was a rich stew of gossip, stereotypes, comments from neighbors and employers, information on whether other people in the family drank or had bad habits, and the like. And none of this could be questioned or cross-examined; none of it was subject to the rules of evidence. Thus one California offender, in 1907, was damned by his bad habits, as recounted in his probation report: masturbation ("since about 14"), and three visits to a brothel; he was also "fond of theatre," and even worse, perhaps, had "no library card."[9] Those offenders who came from "good families," who had jobs waiting for them, and middle-class habits, tended to do much better than immigrants, men from poor backgrounds, or with dubious families, and no prospects in life.

Yet another important reform was the rise of the juvenile court, in the period around 1900. For a long time, many people had felt it was wrong to throw young offenders in with older, "hardened" criminals; prisons were, in a way, colleges of crime. In some states, young offenders were sent to reformatories—specially modified institutions; and there were also special places for juveniles, called "industrial homes" or similar titles. By the end of the nineteenth century, there were no fewer than eighty-eight reformatories in the country.

Nonetheless, when all was said and done, these institutions were still prisons; and juveniles were sent to them after a regular trial in a regular court, with a regular judge, and a regular sentence. The juvenile court—the first one was in Cook County, Illinois (Chicago), around the turn of the twentieth century—was based on an entirely different idea. These were not criminal courts at all. There were no juries, and usually no lawyers. Strict rules of evidence did not apply. The question posed to the juvenile judge was (in theory at least), How can we help this young person in trouble? The juvenile court was not just for delinquents; it also handled abandoned children, children with abusive or neglectful parents, children who were "living in a house of ill-fame," or who were peddling or selling on the streets.[10] And even the children who were offenders were judged by a different yardstick from adults. You could be delinquent without committing any act that would be considered a crime for a grown-up. A child who stole was delinquent; but so was a truant, or one who was "incorrigible," or who disobeyed a parent and stayed out all night in bad company. None of these acts could be found in the criminal code. Adults did not have to go to school or obey their parents.

There is a substantial literature on the "child saver" movement and the rise of the juvenile court. Anthony Platt, in a widely noticed book, argued that the movement was much less humanitarian than it seemed. For Platt, it was more or less a device for asserting control over working-class families. Its basic impulse was "authoritarian"; it created new forms of deviance, and imposed them only on "lower-class families."[11] Platt may have a point. But the records show a more complex and nuanced situation. In California, for example, immigrant parents made heavy use of the juvenile justice system. These were parents who were frustrated and bewildered by Americanized and rebellious children, boys who roamed in gangs, girls who stayed out all night and were sexually active. In desperation, these parents turned to the state. Bartolomeo Comella, a widower, complained in 1907, in Alameda County,

California, that his son Salvatorio, fifteen, stayed out "late at night," and refused to tell his father where he had been. Louise Rolland's daughter was "incorrigible," and, at thirteen, went around with "bad and dissolute characters."[12] All this may well be a kind of class struggle, or class misunderstanding, but of a somewhat different form than the one Platt wrote about.

All of the reforms discussed had one thing in common: they tailored justice to the individual case—at least more than had been true. In general, when the "crime problem" seems comparatively mild, American society shows some willingness to experiment with this kind of penal policy—policy that emphasizes the offender, that individualizes. But when society is obsessed with crime, fearful of crime, when crime is a major political issue, the emphasis shifts back to the offense. This happened, as we shall see, in the years following 1950.

Whatever else the reforms of the late nineteenth and early twentieth centuries accomplished, they were part of a long-term trend to make criminal justice more scientific, more professional. Another sign was the struggle to develop a meaningful concept of insanity. A person can be convicted of a crime only if he or she is sane; but what is sanity? How do we tell when someone is sane or insane? The so-called McNaghten rules, imported from England, defined sanity largely in cognitive terms: did the person know what he was doing, and was he able to tell right from wrong? But specialists in mental disease struggled with this notion, and often found it wanting. Insanity was an issue in the celebrated trial of Charles Guiteau, in 1881.[13] Guiteau shot President James A. Garfield at the Baltimore and Potomac train station in Washington, D.C.; Garfield died of his wounds two months later. By modern standards, Guiteau seems clearly insane, and his bizarre behavior before, during, and after his trial was powerful proof. Insanity was his only real defense, since he was obviously the man who shot the president. Doctors on both sides wrangled and argued; but, as is often the case in criminal justice, in the end it was not science, but the gut feelings of the jurors that counted. The twelve men in the jury room convicted Guiteau; and he went to his death on the gallows.

The power of the jury is even more obvious in cases involving the so-called unwritten law. In 1859, Daniel Sickles, a congressman from New York, went on trial for murder in Washington, D.C. Sickles had a young wife, and the young wife took a lover, Philip Barton Key (Key's father, Francis Scott Key, wrote "The Star-Spangled Banner"). When Sickles found out about his wife's love affair, he went out and shot Key to death. Sickles's lawyers had very few *legal* arguments at their disposal. The best they could do was to claim temporary insanity—a fairly weak reed. But the lawyers did have a powerful *social* argument. Key had deceived and betrayed Sickles; he had seduced Sickles's wife. The adulterer deserved to die. The jury acquitted Sickles in short order.[14]

These cases—and many others—show the full power of the jury under our system. The jury is a most peculiar institution, in some ways. Most legal systems do not use a jury. They pin their faith on professionals—judges with training and experience. Of course, in theory, the jury has nothing to do with legal questions as such. It gets the law from the judge—from his "instructions." A jury is misbehaving—is in fact "lawless"—if it decides, not on the basis of law, but on the basis of feelings, passions, intuitions. But the system is so set up that "lawlessness" cannot be prevented—it cannot even be *detected*. A jury deliberates in secret—behind closed doors. It never gives reasons for what it does. It never explains. Its word comes out as naked fiat. The great sociologist of law, Max Weber, considered the jury system utterly irrational—

not very different from consulting an oracle, or reading the inner organs of birds. Yet a system so structured is not, and cannot be, accidental. It must serve some social function. What the jury does is make possible the application of "unwritten laws," as in the Sickles case. It *is* the voice of the community—a voice harsher at times, more lenient at times, than the voice of the formal law. It is a brake on tyranny at times; and at times it is tyrannical itself—as when southern (white) juries consistently refused to convict men who killed or injured blacks.

Crime has always been a man's game; and it continues to be. Women are often victims, but rarely are they burglars, armed robbers, or murderers. Men kill more often than women, they even kill themselves at a much more elevated rate. It is, and always has been, the men who stab, shoot, and maim each other. Consequently, men go to prison at a rate much higher than the rate for women. In 1899, in Georgia, 71 women were state prisoners, and over 2,000 men. The same was true in other prisons. Imprisonment was also skewed in racial terms, especially in the south. In Georgia in 1899, only 3 of the 71 women in prison were white, and of the men, 1,885 were black and only 245 white.[15]

THE DEATH PENALTY

At the beginning of the nineteenth century there was a strong reaction against the death penalty among people who considered themselves enlightened. The invention of the penitentiary was, in part, as we saw, a search for something to replace putting criminals to death. Many states drastically limited the application of the death penalty, cutting down the long list of capital crimes. In some states, practically speaking, only murder qualified for the ultimate punishment. And a few states (Michigan, Wisconsin) eliminated the death penalty altogether.

There was also a movement—and a successful one—to end public executions. The elites came to consider these spectacles barbaric—appeals to the blood lust of the mob. In the colonial period, ministers and other respectable citizens felt that the drama of a hanging (and a good speech of remorse from the gallows) pointed a public moral. But nineteenth-century elites saw nothing but trouble in these open-air shows. Bigger cities with unruly crowds were quite different from the tiny, God-fearing communities of seventeenth-century Massachusetts. The states began to end public executions—New York did this in 1835. By the end of the century the public execution was all but extinct—at least as a formal, legal device. But in the west it was (unofficially) alive, in the form of vigilante justice. In the south it survived in the hellish form of lynch law. A few states persisted in executing men in public. In fact, the last public execution in the United States was the execution of a black man, Rainey Bethea, on August 14, 1936, in Owensboro, Kentucky. Between ten and twenty thousand people came to see him die.[16]

The legal method of executing people was still the same: to hang them by the neck until dead. After states abolished public hanging, the gallows was normally erected in the yard of the local jail. This was more private than the public square; but still, the yard could hold quite a few people—not to mention boys who climbed tall trees and neighborhood roofs, the better to see the show. Technology came to the rescue, with the invention of the "electrical chair." New York was the first state to make use of this method, in the 1880s; and William Kemmler was the first man to suffer death in "the chair," a dubious honor. The Supreme Court had upheld the state's right to put him to death in this way, rejecting his lawyer's argument that the electric chair was cruel and unusual. In California, each county hanged its own until 1893; from then on, executions were centralized in the state penitentiary at San Quentin.

By about 1920, fifteen states or so had opted for the electric chair. Hanging was on the road to extinction. The electric chair was more private and (in theory) more humane. But the electric chair itself was superseded by the gas chamber; and then by lethal injection. (Utah, curiously enough, retains hanging as an option—another option is death by firing squad.)

The actual use of the death penalty continued to decline throughout the nineteenth century, and well into the twentieth. The trend to limit it to fewer crimes continued. In 1892, the federal government reduced the number of federal capital crimes to three: treason, murder, rape. In the decade of the 1910s, about one hundred people were executed each year in the United States. Later the numbers began to drop. One might have predicted that the death penalty was headed for extinction. As we shall see, this would prove not to be the case.

OPERATION OF THE CRIMINAL JUSTICE SYSTEM

In some ways, it is misleading to talk about the criminal justice "system." The word "system" suggests a certain amount of order—hierarchy, clean lines of authority. In the army, the general gives an order, and the officers under him transmit the command all the way down to buck privates; at all levels, there is no choice but to obey. Of course, the army does not work quite that way; and the criminal justice system is not even like that in theory. In fact, no one is really in charge; there *is* no general. The legislature passes laws, but has no responsibility for carrying them out. The police arrest, but the prosecutors decide whom to prosecute. The prosecutors, in turn, cannot tell the police whom to arrest. Prosecutors can bring a defendant to trial, but the judge can let him go. So can the jury. And so it goes.

Moreover, there is no single, unified system (or even non-system). There are, in a way, three separate layers of criminal justice, at the trial level, one on top of each other, arranged like layers in a layer cake; and it has been this way for a long time. At the bottom, in the basement (as it were) of the criminal court system, are the courts that deal with petty crimes. An endless procession of drunks, brawlers, prostitutes, vagrants, and other small-time offenders parade in front of judges who handle these cases by the hundreds every day. These are the courts of the justices of the peace, or police courts, or municipal courts—the name varies. Process here is quick and slapdash. Lawyers are nowhere to be seen. Small fines and small "jolts" in the county jail are the usual outcomes. In a typical case, of, say, drunkenness, there is a small fine; but many of the drunks cannot pay, and so they work off their fine in the local jailhouse. Mostly, what is punished here are violations against public order—barroom brawls, drunkenness, aggressive begging, soliciting sex, "disturbing the peace"; and the police and judges are like modern traffic cops. Indeed, in the twentieth century, the busiest and most ubiquitous of these basement courts *were* the traffic courts. They process countless thousands of cases, day in and day out. At the absolute bottom—imposing fines for overtime parking—one can hardly talk about "cases" at all. The offenders (and we are almost all of us offenders) get a "ticket," and, grumbling, mail a check to the local court.

Above these courts is the middle layer—the level of trial courts that handle ordinary but serious crimes. Here are processed the burglaries, aggravated assaults, forgeries, and rapes, the cases that are defined as "felonies." A "felony" is a substantial crime—it is hard to give it more of a definition, since each state tends to define "felony" its own way. In Idaho, for example, a felony "is a crime which is punishable by death or by imprisonment in the state prison"; those crimes punished by fines or county jail sentences are misdemeanors.[17] Some states further divide felonies into "classes," depending on how serious the crime and how severe the punishment. Most felony prosecutions—two thirds or so—are for property crimes, burglary, grand theft, larceny, embezzlement, and the like. The rest are mostly "crimes against the person" (rape, robbery, homicide, assault with a deadly weapon). Felony prosecutions are the domain of the jury. But this is a shrinking domain. Most of these cases never see a jury. Trial by jury has long been in decline. In fact, this decline was one of the most striking trends of nineteenth-century criminal justice.

What replaced trial by jury? By and large, it was the guilty plea. The defendant did not go to trial, because he admitted he was guilty; this removed the need for a jury, and for the courtroom battle of the lawyers. Over time, more and more defendants pleaded guilty. Some of these defendants gave up the struggle no doubt because they felt ashamed and repentant; but for the vast majority, the guilty plea was part of a deal—part of the process of plea bargaining. They "copped a plea." The defendant agreed to plead guilty; in exchange, the prosecutor agreed to drop some charges, or to knock down some charges from felony to misdemeanor, or to ask for a milder sentence. The origins of plea bargaining are a bit obscure; it began, apparently, sometime in the nineteenth century;[18] by 1900, in New York County (Manhattan), three times as many felons were convicted through guilty pleas than were convicted by judge or jury.[19] It was always a useful tool for prosecutors, and it became more common in the twentieth century. By the end of the twentieth century, it was positively epidemic; in some jurisdictions, 90 percent or more of all felony convictions came about this way, and trial by jury shrank to a small vestige of itself.

What was the seductive appeal of plea bargaining? Quite simply, it was an enormous saving to prosecutors, in time and money and fuss. For defendants, the appeal was a lighter sentence, or perhaps no sentence at all. But plea bargaining is controversial. It has been attacked from both the left and the right side of the political spectrum. To law-and-order types, it is abominable, because it lets bad guys off too easily (or so they think); to those who are interested in the rights of defendants, it is objectionable because it replaces fair trial with a kind of haggling, invisible, unfair, unaccountable. But plea bargaining is devilishly hard to get rid of. It is at least an attempt to solve a recurrent problem of criminal justice: how to handle routine cases without swamping the whole system. One must not assume that before the rise of plea bargaining there was some sort of golden age of trial by jury. Before plea bargaining, the norm was a trial—but the typical trial was a quick and sloppy affair.

The net result of the rise of plea bargaining, however, was a system far more administrative, far more careless, than the conventional image of trial. That image—and there has been no richer example than the O. J. Simpson trial—fits best a small, select, and important group of trials at the very top of the system. Here due process comes into its own. These famous or lurid cases, dominated by lawyers, leave no stone unturned, and take advantage of every trick of the trade. The jury is meticulously selected. Indeed, this process can take days. At the trial, witnesses parade before the court, and are examined and cross-examined. Ordinary trials, even jury trials, take up very little time; but these cases can go on for weeks, or months. The Guiteau trial lasted for ten weeks;

and one of the lawyers argued his case for five days. These are the cases that give the public its impression of criminal trials; these are the ones the public reads about in the newspaper, the ones they see today on TV. They are important because they hold up a mirror to society. They are dramas—stage presentations, which present society's norms and values in vivid, living form, for argument, and debate.

Perhaps the most famous case of the nineteenth century was the trial of Lizzie Borden, accused of murdering her father and stepmother, on a broiling hot day in Fall River, Massachusetts; their heads were bashed in with an ax. The trial created an absolute sensation; and why? A whole way of life, a whole set of assumptions was on trial. Lizzie Borden was a woman, unmarried, churchgoing, a member of a prominent family. To accuse such a person of so hideous a crime was to suggest a seething cauldron of corruption and pathology under the smooth surface of bourgeois life. It was to suggest that her way of life was in fact stifling, frustrating—that her respectability was a kind of prison that drove her mad. The case forced people to think the unthinkable. It was, in fact, too unthinkable for the jury; Lizzie Borden was acquitted. With the cool advantage of hindsight, her guilt seems fairly evident. What was unthinkable in the 1890s is all too thinkable now.[20]

Other sensational cases have similar characteristics: they put a way of life, a personality type, or respectability itself on trial. Dr. Sam Sheppard, a wealthy suburban medical man, accused in 1954 of murdering his pregnant wife, or, more recently, O. J. Simpson, sports hero and movie star, were two other notable defendants.[21] Other cases appealed to the prurient interests of the public—they tore aside a veil, and showed a fascinated middle-class public forbidden yet strangely appealing worlds of dark sexuality and sin. One of the greatest of these trials was the trial of Harry K. Thaw, who murdered the famous architect Stanford White in 1906; Thaw claimed that White had seduced and "ruined" his wife, the staggeringly beautiful "Floradora girl," Evelyn Nesbit. This "spectacular" case, as a journalist put it, had everything: "wealth, degeneracy . . . abnormal pastimes and weird orgies," and a fabulous cast of characters, from "Fifth Avenue clubmen" to "Bowery toughs."[22]

Most of what the public knows, or thinks it knows, about the criminal trial comes from these sensational trials. But the message of these cases is doubly misleading. On the one hand, these cases give off the message of extreme due process: every *i* is dotted, every *t* crossed, the jury is selected with exquisite care, the lawyers guard the sanctity of the process like dragons posted at the gates, everything is done according to Hoyle and super-Hoyle. That most criminal process is nasty, brutish, and short escapes the public's attention; that most of it is hasty plea bargaining, negotiated by bored or overworked or burnt-out functionaries. The second message, equally misleading, is that justice, though careful, is essentially a fraud. What wins in the end are cheap tricks of the trade. Fancy lawyers, too clever by half, and the flow of money from rich clients: these are what makes the difference. O. J. Simpson walks, although most (white) people were 100 percent convinced he had killed his wife and her friend in cold blood; convinced, too, that the evidence was overwhelming. Cases like this feed the perception that dangerous killers, gangsters, and mafiosi can buy their way out of the system. There is an element of truth here; but the further conclusion, that the system is riddled with errors in such a way as to let too many criminals off, is extremely wide of the mark.

CRIMINAL PROCEDURE

The basic shape of the criminal trial has hardly changed over the years; but nonetheless, there were important changes in criminal procedure during the nineteenth century. The defendant won the right to take the stand and testify—a right that, believe it or not, was not historically his. The rules of evidence became more and more complicated and involute in the course of the century. The American law of evidence is the most complicated in the world. This is largely because of the jury—largely because we entrust certain criminal cases (and some civil ones, too) to twelve laypeople, picked more or less at random. We give the jury enormous power—yet the system does not really trust them. All these rules of evidence are designed to keep dangerous information or misinformation from the jury. Suppose a man is on trial, accused of robbing a candy store. You might think it very relevant to know that this is the fifth time he has been on trial for robbing candy stores; each time before he was found guilty. But the jury is entitled to know no such thing. Only the most carefully screened and purified evidence is allowed to go to the jury. Of course, clever lawyers often know ways to insinuate certain forbidden facts into the jury's ears; but this is a parlous and delicate game.

VICTIMLESS CRIME

The colonial period, as we saw, had a great interest in crimes against morality—fornication, adultery, and similar acts that violated divine law. This interest weakened in the eighteenth century; and even more so in the nineteenth. Adultery con-

tinued to be a crime; but in some states, it was specifically re-
defined as "open and notorious" adultery. The change in definition is significant. The Puritans saw no difference between
sin and crime. Nineteenth-century people were not afraid
that God would turn them into pillars of salt; rather, they
were concerned about the stability and integrity of society.
Hidden, occasional adultery was not a social danger. Open,
notorious adultery—that was another matter. That was an attack on the rules, a flouting and a flaunting; it was this that society could not tolerate. Or perhaps society had given up, as
hopeless, any thought of wiping out vice altogether, and was
concerned only with driving it into a corner, forcing it to lie
low, and thus keeping it within reasonable bounds. We might
call this the Victorian compromise. Keep vice illegitimate;
keep it in its place; make no real attempt to stamp it out. Punish only the most blatant of offenders.[23]

The idea is neither ridiculous nor hypocritical. Take today's laws against speeding. Everybody violates these laws—
sometimes. Nobody expects these laws to be rigorously and
constantly enforced. Mere "speeding" is rarely punished—that
is, driving a bit over the speed limit. What is punished is open
and notorious (and excessive) speeding. The level of enforcement certainly does not wipe out speeding. But if it works as
it should, it keeps speeding within socially acceptable limits.

The Victorian compromise did not last terribly long. In the
late nineteenth century, it broke down, and there was a new,
heightened emphasis on victimless crime. The battle against
immorality heated up. One early sign of the new emphasis on
morality was the notorious Comstock Law of 1873.[24] This was
an act of Congress; its nickname refers to Anthony Comstock, a onetime dry goods salesman who became obsessed
with the idea of stamping out all forms of smut and immorality. The law made it a crime to disseminate what Comstock
and other bluenoses considered "filth" through the mails (in-

cluding any material on contraception). In 1895 federal law outlawed interstate traffic in lotteries. This was the period of a stronger and stronger temperance movement, which ended up with the Eighteenth Amendment (Prohibition), and the Volstead Act, which Congress passed to enforce the amendment (more on this later). In the early twentieth century, there were laws to ban cigarettes; in 1907, Arkansas made it a crime to make, sell, or give away cigarettes to anyone, including an adult.

This was the period, too, in which abortion became a criminal act, though some of the laws made an exception for surgical abortions, performed by doctors, to save the mother's life. Symbolically at least, the climax of the campaign against abortion was the death of Madame Restell, the most famous, and successful, of the New York abortionists. Madame Restell had gotten rich selling "Female Monthly Pills," and catering primarily to well-off married women. Hounded by the authorities, Madame Restell committed suicide, slitting her wrists in the bathtub of her palatial New York home.[25]

This was a period, too, that tightened the legal controls over sexual behavior (or tried to). The age of consent was raised dramatically. This age of consent is a concept in the law of rape. A female below the age of consent cannot legally agree to sexual intercourse. At common law, the age of consent was ten (which seems absurdly low). In the late nineteenth and early twentieth century, state after state raised the age of consent, so that by the time of the First World War, it was eighteen in California and a flock of other states, including Nebraska, North Dakota, and Texas; and in almost every other state, the age was sixteen. This meant that, when two teenagers had sex, the male was by definition a rapist, the female by definition a victim—even if they both were completely willing or even eager to do the deed. Obviously, most teenagers who were sexually active never ran afoul of the law.

Still, the law was far from a dead letter; its enforcement, as always, was colored by the prejudices and presuppositions of the authorities.[26]

This was also a period of intense excitement over the so-called white slave trade—the idea that young, innocent, needy girls, often country girls unfamiliar with the big city, were kidnapped and held in virtual slavery: as one pamphlet, published by the Chicago Rescue Mission, described such an incident, the young girl would be "lured into a restaurant or wine-room," made drunk, "doped sufficiently to become passive," then taken to the "house" and "broken in" in the "most violent and nauseating manner, perhaps . . . the prey of twenty or thirty men"; at this point, "absolutely ruined," she is held captive, and "from that time on until death relieves her, she must receive all comers THIRTY days Every Month" without respite, even "during the Menstrual period."[27] The terror over white slavery was added to a horror over foreign prostitutes, who presumably were steeped in wild, exotic forms of depravity. In 1910, Congress enacted the Mann Act, which made it a crime to "harbor" any "alien" prostitute; more significantly, it struck a blow at the "white slave traffic" by making it illegal to transport any "woman or girl" across state lines for purposes of "prostitution or debauchery, or for any other immoral purpose."[28] The Supreme Court, in one famous case, read this last phrase very broadly. The defendants in the case were two young Californians, Drew Caminetti and Maury Diggs, who had no connection with the white slave trade whatsoever; their crime consisted of taking their girlfriends across the line into Nevada, and having sex with them there. There was no hint whatsoever that the girlfriends were unwilling to go. But the Supreme Court affirmed their conviction. Decisions of this sort opened the door for quite a few questionable prosecutions; the black boxer Jack Johnson was prosecuted under the Mann Act, most likely because his girlfriend was white; and Charlie Chaplin, another notable victim, went on trial because his politics were offensive to the FBI and its grim leader, J. Edgar Hoover.[29]

This was also the period of the so-called red-light abatement movement. This was a serious attempt to close down the red-light districts. Of course, these districts had always operated without benefit of legality; but they were tolerated in city after city. Payoffs to police and politicians were one reason for this toleration. But it was not the only reason. After all, there was (and is) a tremendous demand for "vice." The dives and brothels and gambling joints were full of customers, and nobody had kidnapped *them*. The authorities simply let vice happen. In St. Paul, Minnesota, for example, after 1863 it was the custom for madams to come to police court once a month and pay a fine. A woman who wanted to open a brothel got permission from the police chief, signed a "roll" at police headquarters, and then routinely paid her monthly sum. Other cities, too, had formal or informal ways of regulating what was basically an illegal business: in Atlantic City, New Jersey, brothels were allowed to remain so long as they were "orderly"; in Memphis, Tennessee, prostitutes had to obey the rules—not on the streets after nine, no riding in carriages at night, no minors.[30]

The officials in these and other cities had bought into what we called the Victorian compromise. They felt it was better to control vice, segregate it, keep it away from nice neighborhoods, than to engage in the futile task of trying to get rid of it altogether. But this is exactly what the abatement movement aimed to do. Chicago closed down its district in 1912, after a parade of ten thousand people who demanded a "clean Chicago." Dozens of cities, from Atlanta to Portland, Oregon, and including New York and Philadelphia, did the same between 1912 and 1917.[31] Stringent laws were passed, to have brothels "abated" as "nuisances." Vice, of course, is not so easy to stamp out. The "social evil" had the nasty habit of reappearing, after a decent interval, and after the storm had passed. Probably, in the end, the red-light abatement movement accomplished very little. It was, in a way, one of the last great crusades to save traditional values. For those who upheld these values, far worse things were yet to come.

DRUG LAWS

In the nineteenth century, basically, there was nothing comparable to modern drug laws or the war on drugs. Here and there, one could find laws and ordinances directed against "opium dens" or the like; but this was as far as the matter went. Not that people *approved* of drug addiction—any more than most people approved of drunkenness or other bad habits. But selling or using drugs, as such, was simply not a crime.

Change came in the twentieth century. Congress enacted an Opium Exclusion Act in 1909. The most important step, however, was the Harrison Narcotics Act, a federal statute of 1914. The point of the law, apparently, was to centralize control of drug use in the medical profession. Unregistered persons could purchase drugs only with a doctor's prescription, and only for "legitimate medical use." In *Webb v. U.S.* (1919),[32] the Supreme Court was called on to interpret the law. Webb, the doctor, was prescribing drugs to maintain an addict's habit; a druggist, Goldbaum, was filling these orders. Was this legal under the act? No, said the court; keeping an addict going was not a legitimate medical use, and any doctor who prescribed drugs for an addict was breaking the law. Many doctors, of course, stopped prescribing drugs; and the addict was thus cut off from legitimate sources. The door was open for drug prosecutions; and by 1925, the federal government made 10,297 arrests for violations of narcotics laws.

In short, in the late nineteenth century, and in the early twentieth century, there was a tremendous resurgence of interest in fighting vice, gambling, drinking, and the kinds of sexual behavior that traditional moral codes defined as deviant or forbidden. What brought all this excitement about? There is no clear and obvious answer. There was, of course, a sense of threat that cannot be completely dismissed as unreal. More dangerous drugs were coming on the market. People knew more about venereal diseases, and how they could destroy a family—the problem in Ibsen's play *Ghosts*. The panic over white slavery was surely exaggerated; but obviously there was such a thing as sexual predation. Still, it is hard to avoid explanations that lean more on culture and attitude than on brute, scientific fact. Joseph Gusfield, in an important book about the Prohibition movement, introduced the idea of a kind of clash of ideologies. Immigrants were streaming into the country. Millions of them came from eastern and southern Europe: they were Catholics, Jews, and Eastern Orthodox. They did not share the temperance ideology of the old-line Americans. Meanwhile, droves of Americans were leaving small towns and farms for the cities. The old Americans— rural, Protestant—felt threatened. Their values were endangered. Vice, sin, and debauchery were eating away at the soul of the nation. Ideals of discipline, self-control, moderation, were under cultural attack.[33]

Who was the enemy? It was easy to blame immigrants and the "dangerous classes." But the real threat (and there *was* a real threat) came from more powerful, subtle, invisible forces: the forces that were reshaping and modernizing the world. Traditional society was passing away. This was even true of traditional society, American style, which was much less traditional than traditional society, European style. The *values* of traditional society were also passing away. A way of life that was rural, Protestant, churchgoing, snug and smug, a way of life that had once ruled the symbolic universe—this was in decline. Its own children were abandoning it. And indeed, even in its heartland, rural America, there were signs of cultural breakdown, waves of crime and pathology—suicides, insanity, violent death.[34]

So, arguably, old-line America, besieged and beleaguered, fought back as best it could. The high-water mark of the campaign to save America's soul—no question—was National Prohibition. The "noble experiment" made it a crime to make or sell liquor in almost any guise. Prohibition took the form of a constitutional amendment (the Eighteenth), which went into effect in 1920, and which prohibited the "manufacture, sale, or transportation of intoxicating liquors." Congress also passed a severe law (the Volstead Act, 1919), to put teeth into its fight against demon rum. Many states enacted their own local laws on prohibition; selling liquor therefore became both a state and a federal crime.

It is conventional wisdom that Prohibition was a dismal failure; that everybody drank, and that liquor flowed like water, despite the Eighteenth Amendment, the Volstead Act, and the little Volstead acts of the states. This is an exaggeration. True, Prohibition was widely evaded, especially in the big cities; but it was by no means inert. Nor was it a total failure. Millions violated and got away with it; but many thousands were caught, fined, or even jailed. Prohibition had its side effects, good and bad: less cirrhosis of the liver, fewer deaths from drunk driving—but more deaths from poisoned alcohol. Prohibition put millions of dollars into the pockets of men like Al Capone. It was a marvelous source of illegal money, and municipal corruption. But it certainly made it harder to drink, and undoubtedly stopped *some* people from drinking. Whatever its benefits and costs, in the end it was a dismal *political* failure; and when it lost its popularity, its doom was sealed.

Prohibition died in 1933, when the Twenty-first Amendment repealed the Eighteenth. From then on it was mostly downhill for the campaign to enforce traditional morality. The old virtues still had (and have) enormous resilience and strength; but they definitely lost ground, on the whole, in the last half of the twentieth century. By the end of the twentieth century, the penal codes of the states, especially in the east, middle west, and west, wiped out most of the victimless sexual crimes. Whatever consenting adults want to do to each other is (legally speaking) their private business. Sodomy is no longer a crime in California or Illinois, for example. The old laws—against fornication, adultery, and sodomy— survive mostly in parts of the south. Even there, enforcement is at best sporadic. Gambling was once mostly illegal. Nevada built an economy on legalized gambling, and it had a virtual monopoly on the casino business for a while. Then came Atlantic City, state lotteries, casinos on Indian reservations, and riverboats that were floating casinos. Gambling is now an enormous business—and mostly quite legal. The Mann Act was never repealed; but it has been amended to the point where it means essentially nothing. The Supreme Court has struggled, in a fairly futile way, to define "obscenity"; meanwhile, pornography is not only basically legal, it floods the Internet; and "dirty words" (including two which were once so taboo the great *Oxford English Dictionary* simply left them out, even though these words were familiar to every English-speaking adult) are in books, movies, and magazines (though still restricted on network TV). The war on drugs, indeed, is practically the sole survivor of the hot war against debauchery and vice.

CRIMINAL JUSTICE IN THE
TWENTIETH CENTURY

Crime, like all other aspects of social life, responds to changes in society. This happens in various ways. Social change often leads to changes in the *definition* of crime. To take one example: In the nineteenth century, many states offered bounties for killing wolves. In the late twentieth century, killing a wolf is a crime. In 1900, adultery was a crime in California; in 2000, as we noted, it was not. Or the definition of crime can remain more or less the same, but enforcement patterns may alter: the Mann Act, for example, was eventually changed (and made almost meaningless); but even before these formal changes, the government had stopped prosecuting people who were simply "immoral" and had no connection with the traffic in sex.

In any event, new technology and new social situations create new problems; and the criminal code responds accordingly, with new crimes or new techniques for controlling unwanted behavior. Auto theft replaces horse theft as an issue. More to the point, cyberporn or hacking were not issues for the criminal justice system before the invention of the computer. The automobile, basically an invention of the twentieth century, revolutionized certain forms of crime—including bank robbery. This was also the century of "organized crime," the Mafia, and criminal gangs. Prohibition and the drug wars poured more money into the coffers of the big-time criminals, supplementing the money from gambling and prostitution.

In the twentieth century, too, the federal government became for the first time a significant player in the game of criminal justice.[35] Before 1900, its role had been fairly limited:

customs violations, people evading taxes on whiskey, and offenses on federal territory, for the most part. The federal government did not even have a prison it could call its own until 1891; it boarded out its prisoners in state prisons. In the twentieth century, a rush of new federal legislation added to the number, and importance, of federal crimes. We have mentioned the Mann Act; the National Motor Vehicle Theft Act made it a crime to take a stolen vehicle across state lines. Narcotics cases and Prohibition cases were other fertile sources. In 1910, 15,371 criminal cases terminated in federal courts. By 1932, there were 70,252 Prohibition cases alone. During the Second World War, the federal government prosecuted draft evaders, butchers who sold black market beef, and landlords who violated rent control laws. All of the great federal statutes created or implied new crimes. The federal income tax is essentially a creation of the twentieth century; and tax evasion and tax fraud make more of a mark on the federal dockets than the moonshiners ever did. Dumping toxic wastes into rivers was not a crime until the passage of environmental laws. By 2001, federal crime laws were a significant part of the total criminal justice effort—though still vastly outnumbered by state cases.

Not only did the federal involvement in crime increase; but crime also became a *national* issue—an issue in presidential politics. This was an innovation. Abraham Lincoln or for that matter Woodrow Wilson never talked about the crime problem. Prohibition did, however, focus attention on the role of the central government. President Hoover appointed a commission, chaired by George Wickersham, to study the enforcement of Prohibition, and violent crime in general. The Federal Bureau of Investigation, under J. Edgar Hoover, a master of public relations, represented the entry of the federal government into the law enforcement business. The FBI list of the "ten most wanted" men enthralled the public; in the

1920s and 1930s, "Scarface" Al Capone and other celebrity gangsters, like Bonnie and Clyde and John Dillinger, were notorious figures. People were fascinated by gangster movies, and had a general impression of a wave of lawlessness that only the federal government could hope to contain. Radio, the movies, and TV made local issues into national issues. The explosion of violent crime after 1950 helped put crime and crime-fighting on the national agenda, as well as on local agendas. Crime began to be debated in presidential campaigns. The federal government began to invest in criminal justice—giving grants to local police departments, for example. All presidents of recent decades have felt almost forced to come up with a crime policy; they have felt obliged to make promises to do something about the epidemic of crime. Not that they have much impact, either on the crime rate, or on the system of criminal justice. Crime and crime policy remain, overwhelmingly, matters under local law and local control. But there is more and more of a habit of looking to Washington for solutions to problems. The glaring, unsleeping eyes of the media are focused both on crime and on the federal government; and the public quite naturally connects the one with the other.

The history of criminal justice, after 1950, is dominated by a single fact already mentioned: the enormous increase in crime, especially violent crime. The murder rate skyrocketed in the postwar period. This put great pressure on the political system—and it was pressure in one direction only: toward toughness. An enraged public demanded: lock them up and throw away the key. Ironically, at the very time the Supreme Court, headed by Earl Warren, was expanding the (paper) rights of criminal defendants, the states set sail on a program of tightening laws, building new and bigger prisons, and dismantling some institutions that were tilted too much in the direction of rights and privileges for criminals. This led to such laws as the "three strikes" law in California; under this law, a prisoner convicted of a third serious felony faced, in effect, life imprisonment. Whether this law has had an impact on crime is dubious. It did guarantee more graybeards in prison—it dramatically increased the number of prison admissions of men and women over forty.[36] This brings about, at times, some shocking injustices; or threatens to. In the most notorious case, which made a stir in the newspapers, one Jerry Dewayne Williams found himself facing a possible sentence of twenty-five years to life for stealing a slice of pepperoni pizza from four kids in Redondo Beach, California.[37] In the end—perhaps because of all the publicity—the judge reduced Williams's prior felonies to misdemeanors, and he ended up with a mere two years.[38] Yet even that seems rather harsh.

The indeterminate sentence came under attack; and a number of states abolished it, including California. The demand for tougher and tougher laws fueled the movement to get rid of it. Parole, too, was subjected to blistering criticism. A kind of unholy coalition united against the parole system. Civil libertarians complained—with justice—that there was something quite arbitrary and unfair about the parole process. Prisoners had no voice and no role, nothing like a fair trial; and yet years of their lives hung in the balance. The parole board was accountable to nobody. Those who stood for law and order, to the contrary, felt that the process was too soft, too easy to manipulate. Dangerous thugs were getting out of prison too quickly. What was needed was long, tough sentences—without the loopholes. In an intensely political atmosphere, parole was eliminated outright in some states. Many states adopted sentencing "guidelines," to squeeze discretion out of the system, and to prevent judges from "coddling" criminals. These guideline statutes set up complicated grids, and divided crimes into multiplex categories. In Illinois, for example, there were seven classes of felonies; the judge had a narrow band of choices within each class. Burglary, for example, was a class 2 felony; the sentence had to be between three and seven years—more if the offense was "exceptionally brutal" or showed "wanton cruelty."[39] In 1984, beginning with Washington state, the states also began to pass "truth in sentencing laws." These were laws that required convicts to serve at least 85 percent of their sentence—laws, in other words, that cut down drastically on time off for good behavior in prison. The federal government got into the act by making "incentive grants" (for building prisons) to states that had such laws—which most of them soon did.[40]

All of these factors put together resulted in a huge new nation of prisoners—a whole world of men (mostly men) behind bars. At a time when other developed countries were trying to slash the number of prisoners, the United States was dumping tons of human debris into crowded cells; California, in 1998, had more men and women in jail or prison than France, Great Britain, Germany, Japan, Singapore, and the Netherlands combined.[41] The American gulag skyrocketed—doubled, tripled; passed the million mark, and headed toward two million, by the beginning of the twenty-first century. In 1997, 1.6 million men were in prison or jail, and 132,900 women; another 3.9 million were on probation or parole.[42] Then, in the first years of the twenty-first century, the country seemed to pause to catch its breath. The numbers of men imprisoned in 2000 actually dropped—though only slightly. A few states, too, began to rethink some of their harshest laws, laws that were filling their prisons.[43] Whether this trend would continue remained to be seen.

And what was it like, this American gulag? There were all sorts of prisons, to be sure, from "country clubs" to maximum security prisons—places that were "factories of crime," where violence, extortion, and rape were routine, and where the strong ruled the weak; where inmates who displayed "the slightest hint of vulnerability quickly become prey."[44] Such prisons were like penal colonies—isolated from the world, and ruled by a tyranny of gangs and gang leaders. Riots and disorders were also part of the narrative of prison history. But except for a small band of reformers, easily ignored, and the prisoners' rights movement (which found less and less echo in the courts at the end of the century), there was no muscle behind the movements for reform.

THE DEATH PENALTY

In the first half of the twentieth century, the tide, in the United States, seemed to be flowing away from the death penalty. A number of states had abolished it altogether—Wisconsin, Michigan, Hawaii. In many other states, practically speaking, the death penalty was available only for murder. (Rape was a capital crime in the southern states—basically, for black men who raped white women.) There was a strong abolitionist movement. Public opinion, too, seemed to be turning. In the 1950s, when the Gallup poll first asked about this issue, a slight majority said they were actually opposed to the death penalty. In a famous case, *Furman v. Georgia* (1972),[45] the United States Supreme Court, by the narrowest of margins, gave a tremendous boost to the opponents of capital punishment. The Court threw out all existing death penalty statutes. None of them was constitutionally acceptable. But this was the view of only five of the nine justices; and the Court's opinion was splintered this way and that. There were, in fact, nine separate opinions, one for each justice.

Furman had been convicted of murder in Georgia. In Georgia, and in many other states, the jury could impose the death penalty in a capital case, without any particular guidelines—it was simply up to the jury to decide whether the defendant would live or die. Some of the justices thought this procedure made the death penalty so random and capricious that it failed its constitutional test—one justice (Potter Stewart) compared getting a death sentence to being struck by lightning. Justices in this camp felt the existing system was fatally flawed; but they did not rule out the possibility of fixing it. Two justices felt the death penalty was completely beyond redemption. Four justices felt that even the Georgia statute was acceptable.

Furman stopped the death machine; but only temporarily. The states scanned the opinions for clues, and began tinkering with their statutes. In 1976, another batch of cases came up before the Court. Since the Court felt the death penalty was random and capricious, some states (North Carolina, for one) decided to get rid of the randomness; anybody convicted of first-degree murder in North Carolina would be sentenced to death. The Court struck this statute down; a defendant had a right to be judged as an individual; this blanket rule was unacceptable.[46] Georgia had come up with a different scheme. Georgia divided a capital trial into two phases. First came the guilt phase. Next, if the jury found the defendant guilty, came the penalty phase. This was a kind of second trial, to decide on life or death. The jury could only impose the death penalty if it found one or more "aggravating circumstances," spelled out in a statutory list. If the defendant had killed a policeman, that was an "aggravating circumstance"; or, if he had once before been convicted of a capital crime, that was another. The statute required the jury to consider any mitigating circumstances; and it provided for mandatory review by the Georgia Supreme Court—which could find, for example, that the penalty was too extreme, compared to similar cases. The Supreme Court gave its stamp of approval to this scheme.[47] Many other states took the hint, and drafted statutes more or less like Georgia's. California, for example, has the same two-stage trial. It also has a long list of "special circumstances" that justify the death penalty—for example, killing a police officer, a firefighter, a judge, a juror, or an elected official; murders with a racial motive; or if the murder "involved the infliction of torture"; or if the murderer used a bomb, or poison, or "killed the victim while lying in wait."[48]

The death penalty, then, has been back since 1976; and public opinion, too, has become strongly in favor of it— perhaps as many as four out of five respondents approve. The Supreme Court has decided quite a few death penalty cases—it struck down the statutes that allowed the death penalty for rape; but the core of *Gregg v. Georgia* remains. It is conventional to say that there is a death penalty in the United States, and indeed there is, but the actual situation is much more complex than this simple statement would suggest. In the first place, some dozen or so states have no death penalty at all. Some states have it on the books, but have not put anybody to death since capital punishment was reinstated; this is the case in New Mexico, New Jersey, and Connecticut. Ohio had its first execution since 1976 in 1999. A fairly large group of states—California among them—have hundreds on death row; but execute very few of them. As of the middle of 2001, California had put nine convicts to death; Oregon had executed two, Colorado one. The vast bulk of the executions take place in the south and in the border states—in Virginia, Florida, Missouri, Oklahoma, Louisiana. And then there is Texas, in a class by itself. This one state accounts for more than a third of all executions. As of July 2001, Texas had executed 248 men and women, out of the total of 728 since 1976. The angel of death is particularly active in Texas.

In 1933, one Giuseppe Zangara tried to assassinate the president-elect, Franklin Delano Roosevelt. Roosevelt escaped without injury, but a bullet struck the mayor of Chicago, Anton Cermak, who was with Roosevelt. Cermak died a few weeks later, on March 6, 1933. Zangara was put to death in the electric chair on March 20, 1933. This kind of speed would be impossible today—unthinkable. Men and women sit on death row for years, even decades. In every state, a death sentence is automatically appealed, and except for the men who give up and want to die, there are endless writs, challenges, appeals, habeas corpus petitions, and so on. Congress and the Supreme Court have shown great impatience with the process, and tried to speed it up. So far without much success. On June 18, 1999, Brian Keith Baldwin went to the electric chair in Alabama. He was forty years old, and had been on death row more than twenty years. He had killed a sixteen-year-old girl, when he was just eighteen. But Baldwin's case is hardly unique. The process is so slow that death rows in many states are filling up fast. California has executed only nine; but it had six hundred on death row in San Quentin as of the middle of 2001. There are thousands more in other states. A disproportionate number of them are black. So, too, of the men who are actually put to death.

Poll after poll shows that the death penalty, as we said, is very popular. After the 1950s, the number of enthusiasts spiked upward; this was the period in which violent crime became a major public issue. Huge majorities at least *claim* to approve of putting killers to death. In truth, most of the men and women on death row are not terribly sympathetic. Even die-hard opponents of the death penalty kept fairly quiet when Timothy McVeigh was put to death in 2001. He had, after all, set off a bomb that killed 168 people, including little children at a day care center. Yet by 2001 the hard core had begun to soften a bit. There were a number of sensational cases, where men on death row went free after DNA evidence or some other dramatic turn of events proved they were innocent. The governor of Illinois called for a moratorium on the death penalty. So did the American Bar Association. More people, perhaps, began to wonder how it came about that completely innocent men had been sentenced to death. One answer, if they really wanted to know, was poor lawyering: dozens and dozens of men, especially in the south, were condemned to die after hasty trials; their lawyers were untrained or incompetent, and there was never enough money to do the job right. Still, many states (Texas, egregiously) stubbornly refused to invest in justice rather than in death.

There might be another reason why the public passion for executions began to sag. In the 1990s, rather suddenly, the serious crime rate began to drop. Murder apparently went out of fashion. Nobody was sure why this was happening. Mayors and police chiefs were quick to claim credit, and point to their own brilliant work; but the decline seemed to be occurring across the board, hard to correlate with this or that form of policing, or this or that policy pursued by a particular city or mayor. There were all sorts of other explanations, none of them particularly convincing. Murder was leaving the scene as mysteriously as it had entered.

THE WAR ON DRUGS

One of the main reasons for the explosion in prison populations has been the fervor of the war on drugs. This was a glaring exception to the tendency to decriminalize the so-called victimless crimes. The drug laws have not disappeared: quite to the contrary. They have become steadily harsher and harsher. Sex and drugs have traded places in the legal system. In the nineteenth century, sex outside of marriage, of any sort, was theoretically at least a crime in many states; but it was no crime to buy, sell, or use opium. Today the situation is basically reversed. And the punishments for dealing in drugs are serious indeed. In many states, it is possible to be sentenced to life imprisonment for a serious drug offense. Ronald Allen Harmelin found this out; he was sentenced to life imprisonment without possibility of parole, under Michigan law, for possession of 672 grams of cocaine. His claim, that this amounted to cruel and unusual punishment, in violation of his constitutional rights, was turned down by the United States Supreme Court in 1991.[49] Michigan has no death penalty; this means that slaughtering a whole family, and owning a pound of cocaine, can be treated as equal crimes in that state.

Not only have the punishments gotten harsher, but the law has tended to take away the discretion of judges: many of the drug laws prescribe mandatory sentences, and some of them forbid probation, parole, and other signs of mildness. The federal government spends billions on drug enforcement. Some of it is for treatment; but most of it goes toward punishing anyone who grows, uses, or sells forbidden drugs. Nor is the money spent only in the United States. Billions more are spent in the vain attempt to keep the drugs from flowing into the United States through Mexico or Colombia or the Bahamas or through other pipelines.

RACE AND CRIME

One of the most troubling aspects of the explosion in prison populations is the impact it has on racial minorities. In 1939, 26 percent of the prison population was black; in 1985, 46 percent. Blacks were in jail or prison in 1999 at a rate 2.8 times as great as the rate in 1980; and a rate 8.2 times as great as the rate for non-Hispanic whites. Almost a third of young black males—men in their twenties—were either in prison, jail, or on probation or parole in the 1990s.[50] According to one study, about 85 percent of the black men who live in Washington, D.C., will be arrested at some point in their lives.[51] The death penalty, as we saw, affects blacks at a much greater rate than whites. The war on drugs has an especially heavy impact on racial minorities: whites and blacks seem to have more or less the same rate of drug use, but blacks get arrested, tried, and sentenced out of all proportion. The most notorious disparity has to do with two forms of cocaine, crack and powder. Crack cocaine gets harsher treatment—one gram is, in terms of federal sentencing guidelines, punished the same as one hundred grams of powder. And 95 percent of all federal crack prosecutions are brought against blacks; in Minnesota, in a case that overturned the Minnesota statute, the Minnesota court pointed out that 96.6 percent of those charged under the crack statute in 1988 were black; 79.6 percent of those charged under the powder statute were white.[52]

There is no question that, in the past, the whole system of criminal justice was drenched with prejudice, and not only in the south. Whether this is still the case is a matter of some dispute. After all, today there are black lawyers, judges, and prosecutors, and blacks sit on juries. But in a society intensely conscious of race, prejudice may work in subtle ways, hard to detect. This shows in the controversy over racial profiling, and the "crime" of "driving while black." And crime is also highly correlated with income and class; income and class, in turn, are highly correlated with race.

A NOTE ON LAW ENFORCEMENT

The legal system is full of rules and commands. Most of the job of enforcement—of making sure the law is obeyed—does not depend on the state, the law, the government. What keeps most of us from running amok, from killing and robbing? Fear of punishment, of course, might be, and probably is, a factor; but also because we have been brought up to believe that killing and robbing are wrong; and also because friends and family might despise us, disown us, if we did these things, or we would suffer acute embarrassment and pain. Punishment is, in a way, only an add-on to the powerful work of social norms; an important one, to be sure. Punishment may be especially important, even critical, when the law forbids acts that are morally neutral. Nobody thinks it is morally corrupt to park overtime; probably most people would pay no attention to parking laws, if they were sure they would never get a ticket. If they think the city might tow their car away, they are particularly likely to obey the law. Murder is probably at the other end of the spectrum. No law is 100 percent obeyed, or 100 percent enforced. In some cases, the slippage is almost deliberate. We used the laws against speeding as an example. It is, in fact, by custom, all right to speed a little bit; sixty-five mph really means around seventy. There is no hope and no chance of catching all speeders; and it is not even desirable. Speeding laws are not ineffective, however; they affect the time and manner of speeding, and they probably keep people from going *very* much faster than they do right now. Partial enforcement, we argued, is a method of control. The same is true for many other kinds of law. We mentioned prostitution and pornography. Can we apply the same analysis to rape, arson, embezzlement, and murder? A yes may seem incredibly callous. But somebody has to decide how much to invest in law enforcement—not just speeding, but also how much to spend on the war on drugs, how many doctors to audit for income tax violation, how many men to put in the field to monitor toxic wastes or to patrol the national forests. The level of enforcement is profoundly variable and, like every other aspect of the legal system, a matter of norms, desires, and politics.

NOTES

1. Joseph H. Smith, ed., *Colonial Justice in Western Massachusetts (1639–1702): The Pynchon Court Record* (1961), pp. 235–36.

2. *Laws and Liberties of Massachusetts* (1648), p. 3.

3. Lawrence M. Friedman, *Crime and Punishment in American History* (1993), p. 40.

4. Quoted in ibid.

5. See Marvin L. Michael Kay and Lorin Lee Cary, *Slavery in North Carolina, 1748–1775* (1995), p. 112.

6. Negley K. Teeters, "Public Executions in Pennsylvania: 1682–1834," in Eric H. Monkkonen, ed., *Crime and Justice in American History: The Colonial and Early Republic*, Vol. 2 (1991), pp. 756, 790, 831–32.

7. Friedman, *Crime and Punishment in American History*, pp. 42, 44–46.

8. See Sheldon Glueck and Eleanor Glueck, *Five Hundred Criminal Careers* (1930), pp. 31–32.

9. Quoted in Lawrence M. Friedman and Robert V. Percival, *The Roots of Justice: Crime and Punishment in Alameda County, California, 1870–1910* (1981), p. 233.

10. Laws Ill. 1899, p. 131.

11. Anthony M. Platt, *The Child Savers: The Invention of Delinquency* (1969), p. 135.

12. Quoted in Friedman and Percival, *The Roots of Justice*, pp. 223–24.

13. See Charles E. Rosenberg, *The Trial of the Assassin Guiteau* (1968).

14. On the trial, see Nat Brandt, *The Congressman Who Got Away with Murder* (1991).

15. 2d Ann. Rpt., Prison Comm. of Ga. (1899), p. 21.

16. John D. Bessler, *Death in the Dark: Midnight Executions in America* (1997), pp. 32–33.

17. Idaho Code sec. 18-111 (Michie, 1997).

18. See George Fisher, "Plea Bargaining's Triumph," *Yale Law Journal* 109:855 (2000).

19. Arthur Train, *The Prisoner at the Bar* (1906), p. 226.

20. On the Lizzie Borden trial, see Cara W. Robertson, "Representing 'Miss Lizzie': Cultural Convictions in the Trial of Lizzie Borden," *Yale Journal of Law and the Humanities* 8:351 (1996).

21. On the O. J. Simpson trial, see George Fisher, "Reasonable Doubt: The O. J. Simpson Case and the Criminal Justice System," *Stanford Law Review* 49:971 (1997).

22. Irwin S. Cobb, *Exit Laughing* (1942), pp. 198–99.

23. See, in general, Friedman, *Crime and Punishment in American History*, ch. 6.

24. The law is 17 Stat. 598 (act of March 3, 1873).

25. See Clifford Browder, *The Wickedest Woman in New York: Madame Restell, the Abortionist* (1988).

26. On the age of consent, and its enforcement, see Mary E. Odem, *Delinquent Daughters: Protecting and Policing Adolescent Female Sexuality in the United States, 1885–1920* (1995).

27. Mrs. Jean Turner-Zimmerman, *Chicago's Soul Market* (4th ed., n.d.), pp. 14–15.

28. On the origin, history, and enforcement of this law, see David J. Langum, *Crossing Over the Line: Legislating Morality and the Mann Act* (1994).

29. On the Johnson prosecution, see ibid., pp. 179–86; on Chaplin, pp. 190–94.

30. Joel Best, *Controlling Vice: Regulating Brothel Prostitution in St. Paul, 1865–1883* (1998), pp. 25, 27.

31. Walter C. Reckless, *Vice in Chicago* (1933), pp. 2–3.

32. 249 U.S. 96 (1919).

33. Joseph Gusfield, *Symbolic Crusade: Status Politics and the American Temperance Movement* (1963).

34. This situation is chronicled, somewhat luridly, in Michael Lesy's strange but compelling book, *Wisconsin Death Trip* (1973).

35. Friedman, *Crime and Punishment in American History*, ch. 12.

36. See Greg Krikorian, "3 Strikes Found to Target Older Offenders," *Los Angeles Times,* Aug. 23, 1992, p. A11.

37. Gordon Dillon, "Pizza Case Unlikely Focus of '3 Strikes' Debate," *Los Angeles Times,* Sept. 18, 1994, p. B1. Because Williams grabbed the pizza from the kids, his offense was technically robbery.

38. "Violent Crime Down, No Thanks to Three Strikes," *USA Today,* Feb. 24, 1997, p. 10A.

39. Friedman, *Crime and Punishment in American History,* p. 308.

40. See Bureau of Justice Statistics, Special Report, *Truth in Sentencing in State Prisons* (1999).

41. Eric Schlosser, "The Prison-Industrial Complex," *Atlantic Monthly* (Dec. 1998), p. 52.

42. These figures are from Bureau of Justice Statistics, *Correctional Populations in the United States, 1997.*

43. Fox Butterfield, "States Ease Laws on Time in Prison," *New York Times,* Sept. 2, 2001, sec. 1, p. 1.

44. Schlosser, "The Prison-Industrial Complex," pp. 51, 77.

45. 408 U.S. 238 (1972).

46. *Woodson v. North Carolina,* 438 U.S. 280 (1976).

47. *Gregg v. Georgia,* 428 U.S. 153 (1976).

48. Cal. Penal Code, sec. 190.2.

49. *Harmelin v. Michigan,* 501 U.S. 957 (1991).

50. Alfred Blumstein, "Race and Criminal Justice," in Neil J. Smelser et al., eds., *America Becoming: Racial Trends and Their Consequences* (Vol. II, 2001), pp. 21–22.

51. Friedman, *Crime and Punishment in American History,* p. 378.

52. Michael Tonry, *Malign Neglect: Race, Crime, and Punishment in America* (1995), pp. 188–89.

SIX

THE TWENTIETH CENTURY AND THE MODERN ADMINISTRATIVE-WELFARE STATE

One of the most obvious and salient features of American law in the twentieth century has been the rise of the administrative-welfare state. This means, essentially, a huge expansion in the kinds of things government does, and the way it does them. Government, at all levels, manages the economy, monitors and patrols the behavior of businesses, provides a package of benefits for poor people—or for everybody—and guards the public health and safety. Government, to do all these things, has developed an insatiable appetite for tax dollars. The present income tax was enacted by Congress in 1913. The Supreme Court had declared an earlier version unconstitutional in 1895; the Sixteenth Amendment (ratified in 1913) undid this decision and paved the way for the tax.[1] The rates under this first income tax law were very modest; and only applied to rich people. Only about 2 percent of the population had to file or pay anything at all. During the Second World War, the rates skyrocketed because of the enormous expenses of running a war; now the whole middle class owed income tax. The government began to withhold tax money from the paycheck of ordinary workers. In any event, even when the war was over, what people wanted from government grew and grew; and some way had to be found to pay for all of it: Social Security, a huge army and navy, atomic bombs, national parks, and everything else. Taxes rose dramatically at the state level, too. How else could the schools and the roads get paid for? Most states had income tax laws; and some cities as well.

Nineteenth-century government, as we saw, was (to us, looking backward) small and weak. The federal government was particularly impotent. Washington, D.C., was a town of no great significance; the financial and cultural centers were elsewhere. The states jealously guarded their privileges. What changed the situation, and created a stronger central government, was the rise of a *national* economy. A national economy meant national problems—at any rate, problems defined as national. Congress passed the Interstate Commerce Commission Act in 1887, in response to demands for control over the giant railroad nets.[2] Farmers and small merchants felt they were at the mercy of the big, bad railroads; state regulation was a pitiful failure, because the railroads were beyond the control of any particular state. Only a federal agency had any chance to be effective. The act set up an Interstate Commerce Commission to administer the law. What the ICC accomplished is another story. The railroads were themselves powerful political actors; and they had a tremendous influence over the way the ICC actually operated. But the act was incoherent from the start: it reflected, as all great pieces of legislation tend to do, a compromise between squabbling and contending interest groups; and the result was a farrago of inconsistent aims.[3] Nonetheless, the ICC act was a significant milestone.

Another landmark was the Sherman Anti-Trust Act (1890).[4] This, too, was a reaction to the rise of big business and the threat it seemed to pose to small people everywhere. The archetypal trust was the Standard Oil Company, John D. Rockefeller's huge and monstrous empire of oil. But there were lesser "trusts," in markets as different from each other as whiskey, sugar, and binder twine. Here, too, consumers and little businesses feared and hated the great industrial combines; they had far too much influence on American society and government; they were monopolies, squeezing huge, unjustified profits out of the public; they ruthlessly drove competitors to the wall. The Sherman Act, however, was in a way mostly symbolic. It was a short, bland, empty statement of principle; it declared that "monopoly" and "restraint of trade" were illegal; but the act made no attempt to define these terms, and set up no agency to administer the provisions of the law. "Trust-busting" was left to the tender mercies of the administration (and the courts). At first, nothing much happened. The courts were hostile to the act, and cut it down to size; the federal government was inert. Only in the twentieth century did the act begin to show some teeth and take on powerful adversaries—Standard Oil, American Tobacco; and, much later on, IBM, AT&T, and Microsoft.

Another important new law was the federal Food and Drug Act (first passed in 1906). Its history is instructive. The states, for a long time, had had laws banning bad food and adulterated drugs. In Minnesota, for example, early in the twentieth century, there were laws about the quality of dairy products, vinegar, jams and jellies, honey, candy, and lard, among other things; and a general law against the sale of any food that was "injurious" or contained any "filthy or decomposed substance," or had a "preservative" added to "conceal the taste, odor or other evidence of putrefaction."[5] But the individual states were just as impotent with regard to products sold all over the country, as they were powerless to control the interstate railroad nets. Federal legislation seemed to be the answer; but business lobbies were far too strong for this to happen easily. Even such incidents as the "embalmed beef" scandal, during the Spanish-American War—rotten meat for the men in uniform—did not succeed in breaking the stalemate. Into this situation came a young writer named Upton Sinclair. His powerful novel *The Jungle* painted a horrific picture of life in Chicago's meat-packing district. Sinclair was a political radical. He wanted to stir up the dormant conscience of the country. He wanted to show that big businesses were vicious and cruel to their workers, that poor families struggled against overwhelming odds to make a decent life, in the teeth of capitalist oppression. The novel followed the tragic fate of a family of Lithuanian immigrants in Chicago. It was also an incredible indictment of the meat-packing industry of Chicago, "hog butcher to the world." The packers sold foul, rat-infested goods, made under appalling sanitary conditions. In one particularly gross scene, a worker fell into a giant vat, and his body was consumed by acid and processed as lard. The book set off a tremendous uproar. Sales of meat dropped precipitously. Even the president, Theodore Roosevelt, became involved. A Food and Drug Act now sailed through Congress, as the opposition melted away. The companies themselves realized that something had to be done to restore public confidence in food products.[6]

The law created a new agency, the Food and Drug Administration, to administer the provisions of the act. But Sinclair was disappointed with this outcome; he had aimed, he said, at the country's heart; but, instead, he hit it in the stomach.[7] Perhaps this was what might have been expected. Scandal and incidents are powerful lawmakers; but they work best when they arouse the passions and above all the self-interest of the vast middle class. The country was not about to buy socialism, or anything truly radical; and there was no chance that Congress would enact deep, thorough reforms of conditions of labor. Wholesome food was another story altogether. Mr. and Mrs. America did not relish the thought that their food was poisoning them; and the idea of unconscious cannibalism was distinctly unappealing.

Another noxious scandal produced the next major reform of the Food and Drug Administration, in 1938. This scandal concerned the newly discovered wonder drugs—the antibiotics. The first of these to come on the market were the sulfa drugs. They were sold as pills. The S. E. Massengill company searched for a way to market sulfa as an "elixir," that is, in liquid form, which people preferred to pills. Their chief chemist (a man with a high school education) found just the right device. But he made one slight misstep: 70 percent of the liquid consisted of diethylglycol, which happened to be a deadly poison. When people started dying in droves, the FDA pulled the elixir off the market; but by then, over a hundred lives had been lost, including thirty-four children. The scandal led Congress to make an important change, strengthening the FDA. Up to that point, the agency had had the power to seize dangerous drugs and get them *off* the market; from then on, no new drug could even go *on* the market unless it had been tested and had the approval of the FDA.[8]

The history of the FDA illustrates many themes that are characteristic of the way American law has developed in the twentieth century: centralization (the shifting of power toward Washington); lawmaking and enforcement by boards, agencies, administrative bodies; and the influence of scandals and incidents—and of the media and public opinion—on lawmaking. All of these trends became stronger and stronger in the course of the century.

THE LIABILITY EXPLOSION

The nineteenth century built up a body of tort law that tilted toward enterprise; the judges constructed a network of rules that, in essence, put limits on damages for accidents, at work, on trains, or anywhere. The job of the twentieth century consisted of dismantling this tottering structure; companies became liable for harms done in ways and to a degree that would have horrified Lemuel Shaw and most other nineteenth-century judges.

Product liability is a prominent example. Any discussion of this aspect of tort law has to begin with the great case of *MacPherson v. Buick*,[9] decided in 1916 by the highest court of New York. The opinion was written by Benjamin Nathan

Cardozo. A man bought a Buick car from a dealer; the car had a defective wheel; there was an accident; MacPherson was injured; he sued the car company. Under an older rule (the "privity" doctrine) MacPherson should have sued the dealer—the company that actually sold him the car—and not the company that *made* the car. But in a subtle and crafty decision, Cardozo effectively undermined the old rule: if a product was dangerous, and caused harm, the victim must be able to sue the manufacturer directly. Other states fell into line with *MacPherson*. Suing the manufacturer is now taken for granted. This rule, of course, makes perfect sense in an age of advertising, brand names, and mass production; we buy Buicks, we buy Campbell's soup, we buy IBM computers, and we expect the manufacturer to stand behind his product. Moreover, over the course of the years, the extent of the liability has increased. The maker's liability has become more and more "strict," that is, in many cases, it is no longer necessary to try to show some sort of "negligence" or carelessness. The doctrines are complicated, and the states each have their own version of tort law; but the direction of the trend is unmistakable.

Product liability is only one example of the liability explosion; medical malpractice suits are another. It was always true, in theory, that a doctor, like anybody else, could be held responsible for a careless mistake. But lawsuits against doctors were in fact rare until the middle of the twentieth century. People seemed to be reluctant to sue the kindly old family doctor. Doctors, for their part, seemed to be reluctant to testify against other doctors. But in the course of time, the practice of medicine became more impersonal—and more technological. People *expected* more of doctors; they expected miracles. Or at least they expected cures. The culture of high responsibility, the ethos of "total justice," began to tell against doctors whose patients had bad outcomes. And, as many studies show, doctors do make mistakes—and quite a few of them. Sometimes these mistakes are catastrophic. Another important development in malpractice law was the concept of "informed consent." It is risky for a doctor not to warn his patient that (say) an operation for kidney stones fails every once in a while; or that a certain vaccine has a few rare side effects. If a doctor does not tell all, and get "informed consent" to a treatment or procedure, the doctor can be held liable, even if he or she was otherwise extremely careful, and the failure of the treatment or procedure, and its bad consequences, was nobody's fault.

In the nineteenth century, as we saw, the fellow servant rule effectively choked off the rights of workers to get compensation in cases of industrial accidents. As the country industrialized, the number of these accidents increased enormously. By the end of the century, the toll of deaths and injuries in factories, railroad yards, in mines, and on construction sites was truly dreadful. Organized labor, naturally, despised the fellow servant rule. The courts began to nibble away at the rule, which became cumbersome and riddled with exceptions. Legislatures, too, got into the act; some of them passed laws limiting the scope of the rule, in one way or another.

In the twentieth century, the rule was abandoned entirely. In 1908, the Federal Employers Liability Act eliminated it for interstate railway workers.[10] A later act removed the rule for maritime workers. And in the states, a radically different system, workers' compensation, was put in place roughly at the time of the First World War.

The workers' compensation system was based on an English model, which in turn had been influenced by legislation in Bismarck's Germany. Workers' compensation was a no-fault system. If a worker was injured on the job, he or she had a right to compensation. Fault or negligence was not an issue.

The worker did not have to show that anybody was careless; and it did not matter that he himself was careless. In one notable Wisconsin case, a truck driver's helper tried to urinate off the side of a moving truck—not a wise thing to do. He fell, and was injured; a court held that he was entitled to compensation.[11] Basically, the system covered all job-related injuries. The catch was that compensation was limited. A worker who was totally disabled could recover a certain percentage of salary for so many weeks or so many years. A worker who was partially disabled recovered under another statutory formula. The statutes also typically contained a kind of grisly catalogue of body parts: if you lost an arm, or a leg, or an eye, or a thumb, you recovered so many weeks at such and such a rate: for example, under the current Arkansas statute, an arm amputated at the elbow is worth 244 weeks of compensation; a lost thumb, 73 weeks, a toe ("other than the great toe") 11 weeks; one testicle, 53 weeks; both testicles, 158 weeks.[12]

Thus, in an important sense, this new system was a compromise. The employer lost its defenses—basically, the employer had to pay compensation whenever a worker was injured on the job. But the employer was now immune from ordinary lawsuits. No money for pain and suffering. No jury trials. No chance of some staggering recovery.

Like the law of torts, workers' compensation, once in force, had a kind of life of its own; it also expanded, and in the direction of more coverage, more liability. The early statutes were rather restrictive in some ways: they stayed closer to the classical picture of an industrial accident, and the dangerous world of the factory or mine. The Oklahoma statute, in fact, specifically limited coverage to "dangerous" occupations: blast furnaces, logging, lumbering, and others on a statutory list.[13] The early statutes, too, hardly covered occupational diseases—these, after all, were not "accidents" in the popular sense. Workers who got sick on the job, and from the job, often collected nothing. This was the case of the "radium girls," young women hired to paint luminous dials on wristwatches. They began dying of cancer in the 1920s, but most of them never collected from their companies.[14] The later statutes were much more comprehensive; New Jersey, where many of these girls had lived, amended its law in 1949, to cover "all diseases arising out of and in the course of employment." Workers also began to recover for such things as heart attacks on the job. At first, the courts more or less insisted that the heart attack had to be the result of something special, different, stressful, or unusual—a plain old heart attack was not enough. Some states still insist on this;[15] but the decisions, over time, have become more and more favorable to employees and their families. By the end of the century, it would not be too much of an exaggeration to say that almost anything on the job that disabled or impaired a worker would give rise to a claim. Unlike some European countries, the welfare system of the United States is full of gaps and holes. Tort law, for all its crudity, together with the expanded workers' compensation laws, plugs at least some of these gaps or holes. It is, in a way, irrational that a man who has a heart attack on Sunday, watching a football game, has no claim against anyone; but the same heart attack, on Monday, at lunch at the office, or while sitting at his desk, might give him the right to collect from the boss. But nobody ever claimed that the legal system (or society) had to be totally coherent, totally rational, totally consistent.

It would have been inconceivable, in the early days of workers' compensation, for a worker to claim a right to payments on the grounds that the job had driven him crazy, or thrown him into a deep depression. Or that a worker went into a compensable funk on being told she was fired or transferred to a different job. But these claims began to sprout like weeds in the last part of the century; and many of them were successful. Employers were, to say the least, alarmed; and they ran in panic to the legislatures, begging for relief. Many of the legislatures were receptive; they cut back substantially on the right of workers to make claims for psychological injury. The Arkansas statute, for example, was amended in 1993, so that now a "mental injury or illness is not . . . compensable . . . unless it is caused by physical injury to the employee's body."[16] Something similar—a wave of backlash—took place, as we shall see, with regard to tort law in general.

THE WELFARE-REGULATORY STATE

The New Deal—the presidency of Franklin D. Roosevelt— was a great watershed in the history of the United States, and a great watershed, too, in legal history. There is debate about just how much of Roosevelt's program was a genuine break with the past—how new, in other words, the New Deal really was. No doubt precedents can be found for every aspect of it; after all, as Ecclesiastes put it, there is nothing new under the sun. Nor was President Herbert Hoover—Roosevelt's unlucky predecessor—as inert and uncaring as he has been pictured. But in the aggregate, the New Deal *was* different; and it brought about big changes both in the substance and the culture of American law. Power had been trickling, then flowing in the direction of Washington, D.C.; now it poured in, in a mighty torrent. The states were bankrupt and prostrate. The country cried out for national leadership; and with Roosevelt, it got it.

The New Deal was hardly a single, comprehensive, coherent program. Roosevelt tried this and tried that, sometimes quite inconsistently. The NIRA—the National Industrial

Recovery Act—and the early New Deal in general, took a strongly corporatist approach toward ending the depression. The idea behind the NIRA was to get companies in all sorts of industries to come together, draft codes, cut production, raise prices and wages. Many industries did draft these codes, although the process was bumbling and chaotic. But in the "sick chicken" case—*Schechter Poultry Corp. v. United States* (1935)[17]—the Supreme Court unanimously held that the NIRA scheme was unconstitutional. The statute had given too much power to industry groups; it had, in effect, handed them the right to make laws, binding on millions of people. This was "delegation run riot"; and, in the Court's opinion, a violation of fundamental law.

This was not the only New Deal landmark that the Supreme Court struck down. In *United States v. Butler* (1936),[18] for example, the Supreme Court ended the life of the Agricultural Adjustment Act of 1933. This law aimed at lifting farm prices out of their slump, by paying farmers to grow less and produce less. After losing a whole series of cases, the president became outraged and impatient. The "nine old men" were frustrating the will of the people (and his will, too). Roosevelt was reelected, in 1936, in a landslide. He then came up with a cunning scheme to neutralize the Court. Essentially, he asked Congress to allow him to increase the size of the Court, to give him power to appoint New Deal judges. Perhaps to his surprise, the "court-packing plan" set off a firestorm of protest. Roosevelt had overstepped himself; somehow, he was seen as desecrating a national shrine. The plan went down to ignominious defeat.[19]

But Roosevelt had his way in the end. He was elected four times; he outlasted the "nine old men"; and as the years went by, he was able to appoint justices who saw things the New Deal way. Even before this happened, there were signs the justices (or a majority of them) were growing more sympathetic to the New Deal programs. The later programs all passed the judicial test.

In the aggregate, the New Deal legislation made a real difference in society. The New Deal left a permanent mark on the banking system. It created a system of deposit insurance, to discourage runs on the banks; the government guaranteed the safety of people's deposits. The Securities and Exchange Act tamed the bulls and the bears of Wall Street. Companies that floated stock had to tell the truth about their financial condition. The Securities and Exchange Commission became an important watchdog; investors were much less at the mercy of the robber barons. The New Deal also altered labor law fundamentally. The Wagner Act put the federal stamp of approval on the union movement, and created an agency, the National Labor Relations Board, to make sure employers let workers organize, and played fair during union elections. The Tennessee Valley Authority brought electricity to one of the poorest, most backward sections of the country. Massive public works and conservation programs gave jobs to millions of unemployed people. Works Progress Administration workers built trails, painted murals in post offices, raked leaves, put on plays—but most fundamentally, earned paychecks for tens of thousands of families otherwise on the brink of disaster.

In this economic crisis, a huge segment of the population fell out of the middle class into poverty and distress. Relief and welfare were no longer matters solely for a class of the habitually wretched and forlorn. The federal government responded to the cries of what we might call the submerged middle class. One responsive program was to build public housing—an idea that perhaps would have horrified Hoover. But in some ways the keystone of New Deal policy was the Social Security Act of 1935. No statute in the twentieth century has been more important. This complex law was, in part, a conventional poor relief law; it also set up a program of unemployment compensation, funded by taxes. Most significantly, it created a system of old-age pensions, to be financed partly by employers, partly by workers through payroll deductions. At retirement age, the retired worker would receive a pension. The pension depended, in part, on how much he or she had paid in. It depended in no way on poverty or need; it would go to both rich and poor. These old-age pensions would kill two birds with one stone. Old people who no longer worked would get a check from the government, to keep the wolf from their door. And the prospect of a pension would encourage them, in a time of heavy unemployment, to leave work and make way for younger workers.

Roosevelt's Democratic party had swept the country in 1932 and 1936; but in the American system, losing parties learn to accommodate themselves, and they eventually bounce back. Harry Truman followed Roosevelt; but when he left office, the country turned to a popular war hero (and Republican), Dwight D. Eisenhower. The war had put an end to the Great Depression, and to the depression mentality. The country was much more prosperous; prosperous people, on the whole, tend to be fairly conservative. The Republicans in office left the core of the New Deal intact—they had to. In labor law, and a few other fields, they made some attempt to restore "balance" in public policy. But nobody dared touch Social Security.

Indeed, during the presidency of Lyndon Johnson, in the 1960s, there was a new burst of legislative energy, and a huge new expansion of the welfare state. Johnson announced his Great Society program, and declared a "war on poverty." The "war on poverty" was as hard to win as his other war, the war in Vietnam—which was Johnson's downfall—but Johnson did leave behind him a permanent legacy. He pushed through a bold cluster of statutes—very notably, he created Medicare, which provided free hospital insurance for people over sixty-five.[20] This, like Social Security itself, not only helped them; it helped the next generation. Middle-aged people no longer had to worry about grandma's operation and its drain on their resources. Medicare is now firmly in the pantheon of untouchable programs, along with Social Security itself. Johnson also rammed a great Civil Rights Act through Congress.

The New Deal had been primarily concerned with a sick economy. Economic issues were also very salient in the period just after the Second World War. The GI Bill of Rights, a package of benefits for veterans—free schooling; loans to buy homes—was not simply a matter of national gratitude; it was also a plan to sop up unemployment, and to stimulate the economy. The GI Bill revolutionized higher education; and it helped finance the rush to the suburbs. The government, in effect, gave millions of veterans the power to buy their little dream house in the suburbs. A huge road-building program helped the suburban families travel back and forth to their jobs and their houses. The economy of course is still a major focus of national policy; and always will be. But from the 1960s on, more and more national programs concerned other factors as well—lifestyle issues, social issues, issues of safety and health, issues of the environment. The age of unlimited growth, and unlimited resources, seemed finally over. At one time it felt only natural to cut down trees, drain marshes, kill wolves, and drill oil wherever you could find it, whether in the wilderness or in downtown Los Angeles. But now the marshes had become "valuable wetlands," the wolves were the darlings of the children of mother earth, oil drilling and strip mining were out, historic preservation was in. Not all of this was based on a shift in the nation's aesthetics. In October 1948, the "Donora death fog"—a noxious blanket of deadly air—created darkness at noon in Donora, Pennsylvania, and killed twenty people.[21] The country woke up to the fact that it might choke to death on its own industrial prosperity and poison itself with its own polluted drinking water. Clean air and clean water could not be taken for granted. Programs, laws, regulations with teeth were needed.

To every action there seems to be a reaction; to every "advance" a serious backlash. Nobody wants the California condor to fly into extinction; but should we kill a mighty dam for the sake of some miserable little fish, or steal jobs from loggers because of the spotted owl? The social insurance programs seem solid, politically speaking. Nobody talks about abolishing Social Security or Medicare. But there are grave concerns about how to keep them solvent. In the first years of the twenty-first century, plans to "save" Social Security sprouted like weeds. Ordinary welfare has had a different fate. Middle-class people take their own package of subsidies for granted. They feel they earned this money, by God; they paid for it with their sweat and their dollars. Yet many seem to resent deeply any payments to the poor. It did not help that President Reagan and others portrayed people on welfare as parasites and cheats. Millions of people came to feel that welfare mothers were typically lazy and irresponsible, and immoral besides, popping baby after baby from a series of transient lovers, and sucking up the taxpayers' hard-earned money in order to live empty, fraudulent, dissolute lives. These mothers were, moreover, inclined to be black. Some people sincerely felt, no doubt, that welfare did more harm than good; that it sapped the moral fiber of people who received it, and created a culture of dependence. President Clinton promised to "end welfare as we know it"; and Congress was eager to help him out. Welfare reform had the goal of forcing people off the welfare rolls, and onto the job market. The welfare rolls, not surprisingly, have dropped in state after state; but it is still too early to tell what the ultimate impact will be.

THE CIVIL RIGHTS MOVEMENT

By the end of the nineteenth century, the position of the black population in the south had reached some kind of low point. Most blacks lived in these states, the states of the old Confederacy. Most of them were farmworkers, tenants, or sharecroppers, dependent on white employers. Every southern state had a network of rigid laws segregating blacks from whites—in schools, very notably; but also elsewhere, on trains and buses, and even in prison. These laws expressed a culture of white supremacy. They were part of a social and legal code that made blacks totally subordinate to whites. The Fifteenth Amendment was supposed to guarantee to blacks the right to vote. But the Fifteenth Amendment was a dead letter in the south. In the late nineteenth and early twentieth centuries, the southern states effectively stripped blacks of their right to participate in electoral politics.[22] Through a variety of tricks, some legal, some not, they drove blacks off the voters' rolls. In South Carolina, for example, voters had to pay a poll tax, own property (of the value of $300 or more); and they had to be able to read and write "any section" of South Carolina's constitution. There were tests of this kind in other states, too. Somehow, blacks were never able to pass these tests. If necessary, the southern states used violence to make sure blacks stayed away from the polls. These strategies were—no surprise—extremely effective. In Alabama, in 1906, 85 percent of the male white voters were registered—and 2 percent of adult black males. No blacks held political office. There were no black judges, and only a small handful of black lawyers. All power was in the hands of the white majority.

The criminal justice system was weighted heavily against blacks. Judges, juries, prosecutors were invariably whites.

Blacks accused of certain crimes—rape of a white woman, for example—were practically guaranteed a quick, perfunctory trial; and a verdict of guilty. Justice for blacks was rough, rude, nasty, and deadly. But even tilted justice was not severe enough for many southerners. Lynch law added another layer of terror. Almost three thousand blacks were lynched between 1889 and 1918. Just under 20 percent of these had been accused of raping a white woman (raping a black woman hardly counted). Others were accused of murdering whites, or simply of insolence. Some lynchings were comparatively orderly affairs—if you can call a lynching orderly—but in others, the lynch mob acted with incredible, inhuman brutality, sometimes torturing the victim to death. Luther Holbert and his wife, lynched in Mississippi in 1904, had their fingers chopped off (and distributed as souvenirs), then their ears; before they were burned to death, the mob bored into their flesh with corkscrews. Typically, a coroner's jury either exonerated the lynch mob, or piously proclaimed that the lynchers were unknown—even though lynch mobs usually worked in public, before crowds, and in broad daylight.[23] Rarely was anybody punished for taking part in a lynching.

The federal courts had not been much help to blacks in the south after the end of Reconstruction. Indeed, the Supreme Court had declared one of the key post–Civil War civil rights statutes unconstitutional;[24] and in the notorious case of *Plessy v. Ferguson* (1896),[25] the Supreme Court put its stamp of approval on segregation itself. This was the "separate but equal" doctrine, which legitimated the American brand of apartheid. The situation began to change, though slowly, in the twentieth century. There had always been, in a way, a civil rights movement; always black leaders who protested against segregation. A key step was the founding of the National Association for the Advancement of Colored People (NAACP). This organization began to pursue a policy that centered on the courts. After all, there was nothing much to be gained by begging the legislatures and city councils of the south for relief; they were bastions of white supremacy. The federal government was hostile or indifferent—indeed, Woodrow Wilson, a southerner by birth, was an ardent segregationist. The courts looked like the only hope for some kind of relief.

The litigation strategy, under the leadership of Charles Houston and then of Thurgood Marshall, slowly produced results. The Supreme Court began to back away from *Plessy v. Ferguson.* In *Buchanan v. Warley* (1917),[26] the Supreme Court struck down an ordinance of Louisville, Kentucky, that made it illegal for a black family to live on a block inhabited mostly by white folks; and vice versa. The Court also began to trim the edges of school segregation. In *Missouri ex rel. Gaines v. Canada* (1938),[27] a black man, Lloyd L. Gaines, tried to get into the law school of the University of Missouri; the university refused to admit him, and the state courts affirmed this decision. The Supreme Court reversed—here of course the state could not even pretend that the facilities were separate but equal; they offered to pay Gaines's tuition in some other state, but this, the Court felt, was not an adequate response. There were other cases in which black plaintiffs won, but the Court did not have to address the *Plessy* rule directly. For example, in *McLaurin v. Oklahoma State Regents* (1950)[28] the black plaintiff, George McLaurin, was admitted to the state university, but had to sit in a separate row, eat at a separate table in the cafeteria, sit in a special place in the library. This was hardly treatment "equal" to what white students got. But it was not until *Brown v. Board of Education* (1954)[29] that the Supreme Court took the decisive step of declaring that *all* school segregation violated the Fourteenth Amendment. It was a unanimous opinion, written by the new chief justice, Earl Warren. In some regards, this was a cautious decision: the Court did not order an immediate end to segregation in the schools; indeed, it ordered new argument on the issue of how to implement the decision. In the second *Brown* case[30] the NAACP argued for a sharp, bold order to get rid of segregation; but the Court instead ordered desegregation to proceed "with all deliberate speed," an odd turn of phrase, and essentially dumped the matter into the lap of the lower federal courts.

Brown itself was cautious in yet another way: it confined itself to education. It said nothing about segregation in other areas of southern life. But the Court soon made clear that the principle of *Brown* went far beyond school segregation. In a series of cases, the Supreme Court struck down every instance of official apartheid that came before it: parks, swimming pools, public facilities in general. And, perhaps most dramatically, the Supreme Court in 1967 unanimously voided all existing miscegenation laws, in *Loving v. Virginia*.[31] Loving was a black man who had married a white woman: the ultimate offense to white supremacy. At one time, most states had forbidden interracial marriage; but by the 1960s, these statutes survived mostly in the southern states. After *Loving*, they vanished entirely from the law.

Between 1950 and 2000, race relations in the United States were totally revolutionized. There seems little question that the federal courts played a role in the process. The Supreme Court unleashed powerful forces, and laid the *legal* foundations for a multiracial society. But how crucial in fact was the role of the federal courts? Scholars do not agree. A judicial decision does not arise in a vacuum; it comes out of a context. The years of the Warren Court were also the years of Martin Luther King and a militant civil rights movement. These were also the years of the Cold War; the racial habits of the south were a national embarrassment. The Second World War had been in part a struggle against a racist (Nazi) regime. The old colonial empires were breaking apart after the war; African,

Asian, and Caribbean states became independent. American apartheid was a public relations disaster; when a foreign black ambassador or journalist was insulted in a hotel or restaurant, the United States suffered in the eyes of the world—and the gleeful Soviets won a point in the propaganda game.[32] Meanwhile, blacks had been moving north, where they voted, and had a measure of political influence. White opinion in the north was changing, slowly but surely, in the direction of greater racial equality. President Truman ordered the armed forces desegregated in 1948. Blacks entered major league baseball; they sang at the Metropolitan Opera.

The Supreme Court has no army, no way to force its dictates on society. Whether its decisions "stick," or dissipate in empty air, depends on the reaction of society. The southern states, as a matter of fact, simply refused to obey the dictates of *Brown;* for years, almost no black children went to school with whites in Mississippi or Alabama. The governor of Arkansas, Orval Faubus, openly refused to obey a court order admitting black children into a Little Rock high school. At this point, the president (Dwight D. Eisenhower) reluctantly brought in the troops—he could not allow federal power to be so visibly defied. But the southern states disobeyed as long as they could—and often quite successfully. They dithered and delayed; they fought back in court, they used violence and dirty tricks. In the end, they failed. The forces allied against them proved, at last, too strong.

The role of the courts is open to debate; but the Civil Rights Act of 1964 clearly did make a difference. This act outlawed race discrimination in housing, education, employment, public accommodations. It created a federal agency to enforce the dictates of the law. It opened the courts to lawsuits by people who felt the sting of prejudice. Some aspects of the law were immediately and almost totally successful. Hotels and restaurants could no longer turn away black customers. Housing and employment were stickier subjects; but the act definitely cut down on discrimination, and, at the very least, drove prejudice underground.

The Voting Rights Act of 1965 was also extremely important. Of course, blacks in the south had always had the right to vote—on paper. They lost the right, in practice, as we have seen, through a series of legal maneuvers, dirty tricks, and violence. Since that time, the fight for black suffrage had been carried on slowly, county by county, lawsuit by lawsuit—an almost impossible job. The act of 1965 tried to cut through the technicalities with a bold and novel maneuver. The act contained a "trigger" mechanism: if statistics suggested that a county was not allowing blacks to vote, then the federal government stepped in and guaranteed blacks the right to register and vote. This statute was a death blow to political white supremacy. By the end of the twentieth century, there were black legislators, congressmen and congresswomen, black mayors and city officials, all over the south; and Virginia had even elected a black governor.

DEFENDANTS' RIGHTS

The Warren Court also expanded the rights of criminal defendants—not a terribly popular group, in any period. In *Gideon v. Wainwright* (1963),[33] Clarence Gideon, a Florida drifter, had been convicted of breaking into a pool hall and stealing. Gideon insisted, at the trial, that he had a right to a lawyer. He did, of course—but only if he could pay for it. Gideon had no money, and Florida law made no provision to give him one for free. Gideon was forced to fend for himself. He was convicted. On appeal, the Supreme Court reversed the case, unanimously. The state was obliged, constitutionally, to provide lawyers for defendants who were on trial for serious crimes. Gideon had the right to a new trial—and a free lawyer. This time, ably defended, he won an acquittal.

Equally famous was *Miranda v. Arizona* (1966).[34] Ernesto Miranda, poor, young, uneducated, was accused of rape. The police arrested him, and took him to an "interrogation room," where they questioned him sharply. Miranda claimed he was innocent; but after hours of grilling, he signed a written confession. The judge allowed the confession into evidence at trial and—no surprise—Miranda was convicted.

The Supreme Court overturned his conviction, though by a narrow (5–4) margin. People arrested for crimes had a right to resist police pressure and coercion. The opinion is subtle and in some ways confusing; in practice, it came to mean that the police, after arresting a person, had to give that person what everyone now calls the "Miranda warning." This usually involved some formula such as: "You have the right to remain silent. Anything you say can be used against you. You have the right to talk to a lawyer at any time. If you can't afford a lawyer, the state will provide you with one."

The *Miranda* case was controversial from the start. Nobody questions *Gideon* anymore; but *Miranda* is another story. There were shouts and cries that it tied the hands of the police; that it coddled criminals, at the expense of victims and the public. There were, and are, demands that the case should be overruled. But the case has survived, to this point. *Has* it crippled the police? Has it in fact let dangerous criminals loose? There are those who say yes; but the evidence is murky and conflicting. There are signs that the police have learned to live with it—that it has become part of their culture. Or—which may be part of the same phenomenon—that the "Miranda warning" has become merely a verbal formula, something mumbled routinely, at an arrest; and that the police still have their ways to overawe and manipulate those who fall into their web.

ONE PERSON, ONE VOTE

The Warren Court also acted boldly in an area that touched on the very shape of the political system, in a series of cases on the issue of legislative reapportionment. The first shot was fired in *Baker v. Carr* (1962).[35] The case came out of Tennessee. People who lived in the cities—Memphis, Nashville, Knoxville—complained that the General Assembly was dominated by rural interests; and that the legislature refused to reapportion itself to give city voters their fair share of the seats. The defense was very simple: these were "political questions" and none of the Court's business; indeed, the Court had in the past been reluctant to intervene in such "political questions." But this was a different Court; and in *Baker v. Carr*, the Court jumped in feet first. The case did not actually change the makeup of the Tennessee legislature; the Court simply said that the courts should not duck, weave, and dodge—they had a right to hear and decide. Within a year, lawsuits were filed in most of the states, complaining about methods of districting. Eventually, the Supreme Court expanded and explained what it was doing; it overturned house after house, legislature after legislature, and applied a bold doctrine that is often summed up (a bit misleadingly) as "one man, one vote." Both houses of the legislature, in all the states, must be more or less fairly apportioned.

THE AGE OF PLURAL EQUALITY

The Warren Court thus made many dramatic moves during the 1950s and 1960s. If we put them together, we see definite patterns. This was an age that expanded the very concept of equality. This had always been an important American idea—that all men are created equal. But "equal" did not apply to everybody—certainly not to blacks; nor to women as well. And "equality" meant, at best, freedom within a country that was in a way owned and run by and for a single dominant group: white Protestant males.

In the year 2001, it is hard to write a phrase like "white Protestant males" without an implied sneer, or, at the least, the notion that something was wrong, that "white Protestant males" were oppressors, men who ran a regime of domination and hypocrisy. But in some respects this is a bit unfair. Certainly, compared to the tyrannies, past and present, especially those that crept out of the sewers of the twentieth century like so many venomous snakes, the country *was* democratic. It *tolerated* minority religions; there was freedom of speech, and there were no political prisoners to speak of. Part of the reason that the "white Protestant males" of the past have fallen into disrepute is that the late twentieth century made obsolete, and went beyond, their notion of equality. The new age demanded an end to domination by a single moral or ideological system, a single race, gender, language, and way of life, even though much of the domination was cultural, not physical; symbolic, not instrumental. The new notion, which we might call "plural equality," meant power-sharing—both with respect to power in the literal sense, and in the symbolic and cultural senses as well.

Race was the most shining example of plural equality in action—blacks led the civil rights movement, then Hispanics, Asians, and Native Americans joined the parade. With regard to each of these, the American record had been dismal, to say the least. There is no worse blot on American history. The most notorious case, of course, was black slavery, and the virtual slavery of the post-Reconstruction south. But there was rank discrimination against Hispanics throughout the south-west. The Chinese were the object of intense hatred in California; and the first immigration restrictions were directed against the Chinese. The attack on race discrimination benefited all minority races. The treatment of Native Americans verged at times on outright genocide. But now law (and society) came to respect the religions and languages of, say, the Cherokee and Navajo. Gone are the infamous boarding schools, and the attempts to stamp out native cultures because they were pagan and "primitive." The tribes now enjoy a great deal of actual autonomy. White supremacy, in general, has gone underground; and what was once orthodox doctrine throughout the south is now confined to a lunatic fringe holed up in cabins in Idaho and Montana. Racism, to be sure, is far from dead; it is a wounded snake whose fangs are still deadly, as it thrashes about in (what we hope are) the agonies of death.

As important, perhaps, as the movement to equalize races was the movement to equalize the rights and positions of women and men. The Civil Rights Act of 1964 outlawed discrimination against women in the workplace. The story (or legend) is that southerners, bitterly opposed to the law, smuggled sex discrimination into the text; *this*, they thought, would kill the whole idea. If this was their aim, it backfired; the law passed with sex discrimination part of its primal language. But the women's movement did not rise and fall on such accidents of time and place. Gender relations were in process of volcanic change. Women at work, the pill, the success of the civil rights movement—whatever the underlying bases, the effect on society, on family life, on the economy, was stark and dramatic; and the effect on the legal order, necessarily, was of equally dramatic scope.

In 1971, the Supreme Court, as if awakening from a long sleep, "discovered" gender discrimination as a forbidden act, under the Fourteenth Amendment to the Constitution—an idea that would have surprised the men (and they were all men) who drafted the text. The occasion was an obscure case out of Idaho, *Reed v. Reed*,[36] and the issue was a law that gave males preference over females in handling estates of people who died without a will. The case itself probably affected at most a few dozen people; but the principle was revolutionary. The court followed up with case after case that, on the whole, hammered home the principle that men and women had to be equally treated under law. The courts outlawed overt discrimination; and they also got rid of "protective" laws, which feminists considered, with considerable logic, to be (as the phrase went) less a pedestal than a cage. Two generations earlier, most women, and most progressives, cheered when the Supreme Court upheld some of these laws: those, for example, that ordered minimum wages and maximum hours for women.[37] Today, these laws would be out of the question; and their language, all about the delicacy of women, their need for protection, and the glories of motherhood, make the modern reader wince.

The Court played a role in dismantling sex discrimination; but here, too, the Civil Rights Act, in the end, was far more important than any single decision of the Court, and probably more important than all of them together. For one thing, the law created an agency, set up a structure, and opened the door to complainants who felt the sting of discrimination. Thousands of complaints were filed, and continue to be filed, each year. Courts and agencies broke down barrier after barrier: women joined police and fire departments, became baseball umpires and coal miners. The courts and agencies have refused to accept excuses; have sneered at the lame reasons given why women were not suitable for this or that line of work. It was not a one-way street. Airlines were told they had to hire men as well as women for jobs as flight attendants. A nursing school was told it could not turn down an applicant simply because he was male. Another important move was to define sexual harassment as a kind of sex discrimination. Men who groped or propositioned the women who worked for them, or with them, and companies that allowed this to happen, found themselves in legal difficulty. Women were complaining, too, about "hostile" workplaces: sites where they were insulted or exposed to male crudity and anger.[38]

Group after group pushed forward to claim its place in the sun. Very notable was the revolt of the so-called sexual minorities—gays and lesbians. Despite savage rearguard action, they made a good deal of progress. A series of dramatic cases opened the door to expansion of the rights of prisoners as well. Federal courts declared whole state systems of prisons unconstitutional, because of filth, neglect, and brutality. There were also cases on students' rights. In *Tinker v. Des Moines Independent Community School District* (1969),[39] students in a Des Moines high school wore black armbands to school, to show what they thought of the war in Vietnam. This display was against school policy; the students were sent home and suspended. The Supreme Court sided with the students: young people do not "shed their constitutional rights to freedom of speech or expression at the schoolhouse gate."

The Age Discrimination in Employment Act was another product of the 1960s.[40] It became illegal to discriminate against men and women over forty (and under sixty-five) in hiring, firing, or conditions of work. A later amendment (in 1978) raised the upper age to seventy; a still later amendment (1986) removed the age cap altogether.[41] This, in effect, abolished mandatory retirement. A person able and willing to work at seventy, eighty, ninety, or even one hundred cannot be dismissed from the job simply because of a flat rule that counts the candles on her birthday cake. The Americans with Disabilities Act, passed at the beginning of the 1990s, extended the job rights of those millions of Americans who were blind, deaf, in a wheelchair, or otherwise "handicapped."[42]

Restaurants and the like were not to discriminate; trains and buses had to be fitted to accommodate these people. Nor was an employer to refuse to hire a person because of disabilities, if she could do the work (no blind cab drivers, of course); and, in addition, an employer was supposed to make "reasonable accommodations" (ramps, for example), so that a disabled person could actually do the job.

These laws are powerful, and to a degree quite effective. Thousands of complaints pour in to the civil rights agencies—federal and state—every year. In real life, race and sex discrimination have certainly declined since the 1950s; but claims show no signs of abating. Most of these claims never get very far, to be sure. But enough of them flow into the various agencies to generate a huge body of rules and decisions; and enough of them, too, spill over into the courts to make this a vibrant, growing field of law.

The Constitution, that ancient document, now flexed its muscles, and spread its wings over every aspect of American life. From the outside, it looked like a judicial revolution: a wildly inventive and proactive court system, intent on imposing its progressive views on the country as a whole. But this is profoundly misleading. The courts followed as much as they led. Before you can have a *Tinker* case, you must have a Tinker: you must have rights-conscious, rebellious, feisty human beings who have a sense of what is due to them, and are willing to struggle for their goals. And before you can have these rebels, you must have the right norms, the right zeitgeist. A gay rights movement, or a prisoners' rights movement, or a drive against mandatory retirement, would have been unthinkable, and totally hopeless, in the nineteenth century.

THE RIGHT OF PRIVACY

The so-called right of privacy—at least in its constitutional form—got its start in 1965, in *Griswold v. Connecticut*.[43] To be sure, there had been a few hints and suggestions in the case law before that. The issue in *Griswold* was a statute that made it impossible (legally, at least) to sell contraceptives in the state of Connecticut, and even to give family planning advice. The Supreme Court struck down the statute, claiming, in one of its periodic spasms of discovery, that an implicit right of "privacy" was buried somewhere in the text of the Fourteenth Amendment, and in other places in the Constitution. The *Griswold* case talked about the sacredness of marriage, and the possibility that the police could invade its sacred "precincts," looking for evidence of contraception. But later cases made it clear that marriage was not the essential point; personal choices about sex and lifestyle were not a privilege only married people were allowed to enjoy. The climax of the line of privacy cases came in 1973, in the case of *Roe v. Wade*.[44]

The issue in the case was abortion. "Jane Roe" (a pseudonym for a woman named Norma McCorvey) challenged Texas's law, which was extremely restrictive; there was another challenge, to a somewhat more liberal law from Georgia. In the background, of course, was the so-called sexual revolution; and a vibrant and militant women's movement. Illegal abortions were common in many parts of the country; and they often had tragic outcomes. But there was also a larger issue at stake: in her argument before the Supreme Court, Sarah Weddington announced that "one of the purposes of the Constitution was to guarantee to the individual the right to determine the course of their own lives."[45]

Of course, this was not the "legal" issue; nor is it literally true, as a matter of history, that this is what the Constitution was about. But this is how the constitutional *system* had come to be understood by millions of people; and it was the issue that haunted the case, and that led to the 7–2 decision. In essence, the case held that a woman had a constitutional right to have an abortion; to decide to carry a child or not to—at least in the early months of her pregnancy.

The case, of course, has been controversial since the day it was issued by the Supreme Court. Justice Blackmun, who wrote the majority opinion, almost certainly thought he was crafting a compromise—between women's groups who wanted an absolute right to abortion, up to the moment of birth; and those who considered abortion murder, to be banned in all events. Under *Roe v. Wade,* the absolute right was confined to the first trimester of pregnancy; in the second trimester, the states were allowed to regulate abortion, and in the third trimester (presumably) it could be banned altogether.

No doubt the Court expected controversy. Probably they also expected the furor to die down after a while. *Brown v. Board of Education* was even more revolutionary, and created even more of an uproar—to the point of bloodshed; but by the 1970s *that* uproar had abated, and the case had become sacred, untouchable. *Roe v. Wade* has had a very different fate. Abortion, after all, was also a *religious* issue. It remains an article of faith for millions that abortion is murder; and that, therefore, *Roe v. Wade* is an utter abomination. The Republican party, at one point, declared it to be party policy to get rid of the decision. Congress—and the courts—chipped away at the holding. Federal funding for abortions? No, according to the so-called Hyde Amendment, which barred federal Medicaid funds for abortions, except to save the life of the mother, or in cases of incest or rape. The Supreme Court upheld the

Hyde Amendment, in 1980.[46] The Supreme Court, in a more conservative mood, began to show grave doubts about its own handiwork. At one point, the case seemed doomed to be overruled; and it was saved by the narrowest of margins.[47] In 2002 the decision seems secure—for the moment; but two or so appointments of "right-to-lifers" to the highest court might mean the end for this embattled decision.

The court talks about the right to "privacy," but this is a rather odd use of the word. The older use of the term, "right of privacy," had quite a different meaning. If a company, for example, used my picture in an ad, without my permission, that would violate my right to privacy. But the *constitutional* right to privacy is not a right to anonymity, to "privacy" in this sense. It is, in some ways, the opposite—or can be. It is the right to make life choices, about sex, marriage, and intimate affairs, without government interference or disapproval. It is related, in other words, to the reform of laws about victimless crimes. It is a product, in part at least, of the so-called sexual revolution.

Roe v. Wade was a kind of high-water mark. The Supreme Court seemed unwilling to take further steps in the direction of expanding the right to other life choices. In *Bowers v. Hardwick* (1986),[48] the Court considered a Georgia statute that made sodomy a crime—a statute that had analogs in about half the states. The defendant was a gay man, caught in the act. He fought the case all the way up to the Supreme Court. The Supreme Court upheld the statute—by a narrow 5–4 margin. Under the Georgia law, it was a crime to commit "any sexual act involving the sex organs of one person and the mouth or anus of another." This law applied to both gay and straight sex. The court, however, ignored this fact, and insisted there was no "right of privacy" for "homosexual sodomy."

In the last decades of the twentieth century, the Supreme

Court, and the federal courts in general, became more cautious about creating new rights and extending the reach of old ones. Twelve years of conservative presidents put a definite stamp on the federal judiciary. This led liberal interest groups to turn more attention to state courts. In some cases, this technique was brilliantly effective. The Supreme Court of Kentucky, in 1993, struck down the Kentucky law against "deviate sexual intercourse."[49] The defendant in the case, Jeffrey Wasson, had the bad luck to proposition a man in a parking lot who turned out to be an undercover officer. The Kentucky court found the *state* right of privacy broader than the federal right. And, rather ironically, in 1998, the Georgia Supreme Court voided the very same sodomy statute that the Supreme Court had upheld in *Bowers v. Hardwick.*[50] Though it passed the test of the federal Constitution, it fell afoul of the Georgia constitution—at least according to the Georgia Supreme Court, which, after all, has the final word on this particular subject.

On the whole, however, despite some backing and filling, most of the decisions of the Warren Court have stood the test of time. Warren Burger replaced Earl Warren; President Richard Nixon chose Burger specifically with the notion of tilting the Supreme Court to the right. Nixon also had the chance to put other conservatives on the Court. He was, in the main, successful; and President Carter, the next Democratic president, was one of the few presidents who had no vacancies on the Court to fill. Then came twelve years of conservative hegemony. Still, it was the Burger Court that decided *Roe v. Wade;* and Burger himself was part of the majority in that case. The Rehnquist Court was even more conservative than the Burger Court; and few justices have been as conservative as Rehnquist himself, Antonin Scalia, and Clarence Thomas. Nonetheless, at the end of the twentieth century, the work of the Warren Court remained standing, bloody but essentially unbowed.

"Conservative" and "liberal," after all, are relative terms. Few justices have been as "conservative" as Clarence Thomas, but Clarence Thomas is black; and black and white conservatives alike are more liberal on some issues (race is one of them) than even the most liberal judges of the nineteenth century were. Thomas is, moreover, a black man married to a white woman—and this would have made both of them felons in the south a generation or so ago. The conservatives would like to turn some power back to the states, and reduce the size of government. But what they can accomplish is strictly limited. Humpty-Dumpty cannot be put together again. The welfare-regulatory state is the product of profound social forces; it is a genie that cannot be wished back into its bottle.

NOTES

1. The case in question was *Pollock v. Farmers' Loan and Trust Company*, 157 U.S. 429, 158 U.S. 601 (1895).

2. 24 Stat. 379 (act of Feb. 4, 1887).

3. On this point, see Stephen Skowronek, *Building a New American State: The Expansion of National Administrative Capacities, 1877–1920* (1982), ch. 5.

4. 26 Stat. 209 (act of July 2, 1890).

5. Minn. Stats. 1905, sec. 1771, p. 356.

6. Lawrence M. Friedman, *American Law in the Twentieth Century* (2002), pp. 60–61. The statute (Food and Drug Act) is 34 Stat. 768 (act of June 30, 1906).

7. Upton Sinclair, *American Outpost: A Book of Reminiscences* (1932), p. 154.

8. See Charles O. Jackson, *Food and Drug Legislation in the New Deal* (1970), chapter eight.

9. 217 N.Y. 383, 111 N.E. 1050 (1916).

10. 35 Stat. 65 (act of Apr. 22, 1908); an earlier act had been declared unconstitutional.

11. *Karlslyst v. Industrial Commission,* 11 N.W. 2d 179 (Wisc., 1943).

12. Ark. Code Ann., sec. 11-90521 (1999).

13. Okla. Comp. Stats. 1926, secs. 7283, 7284, pp. 662–63.

14. See Claudia Clark, *Radium Girls: Women and Industrial Health Reform, 1910–1935* (1997).

15. Thus, the Arkansas statute quoted above makes a heart condition compensable "only if . . . an accident is the major cause." Sec. 11-9-114.

16. Ark. Code Ann. sec. 11-9-113 (1999).

17. 295 U.S. 495 (1935).

18. 297 U.S. 1 (1936).

19. See, on this, William E. Leuchtenberg, *The Supreme Court Reborn: The Constitutional Revolution in the Age of Roosevelt* (1995).

20. 79 Stat. 286 (act of July 30, 1965).

21. See Edwin Kiester, Jr., "A Darkness in Donora," *Smithsonian,* Nov. 1, 1999.

22. See, in general, Michael Perman, *Struggle for Mastery: Disfranchisement in the South, 1888–1908* (2001).

23. The material on lynching is taken from chapter six of Leon Litwack's *Trouble in Mind: Black Southerners in the Age of Jim Crow* (1998).

24. In the so-called Civil Rights Cases, 109 U.S. 3 (1883); this case voided the Civil Rights Act of 1875, which prohibited racial discrimination in public accommodations.

25. 163 U.S. 537 (1896).

26. 245 U.S. 60 (1917).

27. 305 U.S. 337 (1938).

28. 339 U.S. 637 (1950).

29. 347 U.S. 483 (1954).

30. 349 U.S. 294 (1955).

31. 388 U.S. 1 (1967).

32. See Mary L. Dudziak, *Cold War Civil Rights: Race and the Image of American Democracy* (2000).

33. 372 U.S. 335 (1963).

34. 384 U.S. 436 (1966).

35. 369 U.S. 186 (1962).

36. 404 U.S. 71 (1971).

37. One of the most famous of these was *Muller v. Oregon*, 208 U.S. 412 (1908).

38. On these developments, see Friedman, *American Law in the Twentieth Century*, pp. 305–10.

39. 393 U.S. 503 (1969).

40. 81 Stat. 602 (act of Dec. 15, 1967).

41. Interestingly, the effective date this noble law was to go into effect was postponed seven years for university and college teachers; after that they were covered.

42. 104 Stat. 327 (act of July 26, 1990).

43. 381 U.S. 479 (1965).

44. 410 U.S. 113 (1973).

45. Quoted in David J. Garrow, *Liberty and Sexuality: The Right to Privacy and the Making of Roe v. Wade* (1994), p. 525.

46. The case was *Harris v. McRae*, 448 U.S. 297 (1980).

47. *Planned Parenthood of Southeastern Pennsylvania v. Casey*, 505 U.S. 833 (1992).

48. 478 U.S. 186 (1986).

49. *Commonwealth v. Wasson*, 842 S.W. 2d 487 (Ky. S. Ct. 1993).

50. *Powell v. State*, 270 Ga. 327, 510 S.E. 2d 18 (1998).

SEVEN

AMERICAN LAW
AT THE DAWN
OF THE TWENTY-FIRST
CENTURY

At the beginning of the new century, it continues to be true that law, legal process, and the legal system are pervasive, and overwhelmingly important, in American society. Why should this be the case? We have explored some reasons already. A complex, heterogeneous society, a society in which people are constantly interacting with strangers, are constantly dependent on strangers, a society transformed by modern technology—this is, necessarily, a society that relies heavily on processes of law to govern itself. The same is true of all modern societies—Finland, Japan, New Zealand, Israel; perhaps it is especially true of the United States, because it is bigger than almost all the others, and more complicated, more diverse; and because of a long tradition of reliance on law and legal process; and, for that matter, on lawyers.

At the beginning of this book, we mentioned the thousands and thousands of laws and rules in effect in the United States. Throughout the century, the process continued: more and more legislation, more and more administrative agencies, more and more rules and regulations. The Code of Federal Regulations, which, as its title suggests, lists all the rules of the federal agencies, consists of shelf after shelf of densely packed material. Some of the rules are broad and general; others are incredibly detailed. Anybody who imports an ostrich "exceeding 36 inches in height or 30 pounds in weight" has to have it inspected by a veterinarian, either at New York, New York, or Stewart Airport in Newburgh, New York; this is a rule of the Animal and Plant Health Inspection Service of the Department of Agriculture.[1] Other rules of the APHIS cover every conceivable animal, including the hippopotamus and the tenrec. A rule of the Food and Drug Administration spells out the conditions under which "acrylate-acrylamide resins" and "modified polyacrylamide resin" may be safely used in food.[2] A rule of the Equal Employment Opportunity Commission forbids employers from forcing employees "to speak only English at all times in the workplace"; such an order would be "burdensome" and result in a "discriminatory workplace environment"; it is not allowed unless "justified by business necessity."[3]

Behind each rule is some more general *policy.* The EEOC rule derives from the law that forbids discrimination on the basis of national origin. The FDA is supposed to guarantee the safety of food products. There are also health reasons to inspect exotic animals at ports of entry. You cannot run a regulatory state on generalities. The FDA *must* hire chemists, and specify the exact chemicals that can and cannot be used, and precisely enough so that a food manufacturer can know exactly what to do. The more that Congress lays down general policies, the more the agencies must draft specific rules.

The agencies are run by human beings. They make mistakes. Undoubtedly, many of the rules are stupid and wrongheaded. A great deal depends on how they are enforced—whether the agencies crack a whip, or gently nudge people toward compliance. Most of the tens of thousands of rules are not directly addressed to the general public. You and I do not manufacture automobiles, or slaughter animals for meat, or build skyscrapers. Corporations and other businesses have to cope with most of the rules. There is a never-ending struggle, in which lobbyists play a big role, over the rules. Ideally, the rules should be fair to business *and* the public, neither too harsh nor too lax. The results often fall far short of this ideal.

THE LEGAL PROFESSION

The sheer size of the legal profession is an important sign of the crucial role of law in this society. There are about a million lawyers in the United States. It is by far the largest legal profession in the world. At the beginning of the twentieth century, there were about 100,000 lawyers. The twentieth century has been a century of fantastic growth in the profession.

The United States has always had a big contingent of lawyers, compared to other countries, at least since independence. The United States was, after all, the first middle-class country. In contrast to England, where a tiny percentage of the population—the landed gentry—owned almost all of the land, and pretty much everything else, millions of people in the United States owned a farm, or a lot in the city, or a small shop in town. These millions of people were in the market for simple legal services: help with wills and mortgages, or collecting debts, or buying and selling land. As the country industrialized, businesses big and small developed an appetite for lawyers as well. Lawyers in the United States were not primarily scholars or intellectuals; they were ambitious, pushy young men; they were nimble, supple problem-solvers; they knew how to make themselves useful, how to squeeze themselves into every crack and cranny of the market for information. This was true both then and now. Indeed, in recent decades, the number of lawyers has zoomed upward even more dramatically—growing nearly as fast as the number of computer programmers (or convicted felons). In a society where "law" is everywhere, there is everywhere a need for people who know how to use or abuse it.

So much for the demand side. On the supply side, there

were fewer barriers to entry than in most other countries. For most of the nineteenth century, it was easy to become a lawyer. Most lawyers learned their trade as apprentices—they were gofers in the offices of established lawyers; here they picked up scraps of information, read law books, copied documents, and made themselves generally useful.[4] After doing this sort of thing for a year or two, the fledgling would usually go to a local judge, answer a few questions, and that was that. The tyranny of the bar exam lay in the future. In civil law countries, law was a much more serious business, scholastically speaking. It was taught in universities, heavily encrusted with theory and logic. This was not the common law tradition. There were law schools in the nineteenth century in the United States, but they were anything but intellectual. They were basically cram courses in law, given in the form of lectures. And they trained only a small percentage of the bar.

Eighteen seventy was a year of revolution in legal education. It was the year Harvard Law School got a bold new dean, Christopher Columbus Langdell. Langdell changed legal education dramatically. He aimed to teach law as a "science." He replaced dry lectures with the give-and-take of the Socratic method, and compiled the first "casebooks" to be used as vehicles for teaching the law. He also invented the law professor, in a way. Before Langdell, law schools brought in established lawyers and judges to give lectures part-time. Langdell hired young, smart men, with little or no experience in the world, but skill at teaching—at least in teaching as Langdell thought things should be taught. The Harvard method of question and answer, of plowing through casebooks, was slow and intensely impractical; even at Harvard, it had its enemies. Yet by the early twentieth century, it had conquered all its rivals. Apprenticeship, too, was on the road to extinction. Perhaps what killed it was the rise of the law firm, and the revolution in the way offices were organized: with secretaries, dictation, typewriters, telephones. These "modern" offices sharply distinguished between professional staff and office staff; the apprentice, who was a little of both, became obsolete. The Langdell method, too, with its pretension to science and rigor, brought prestige to law teaching. Whether students learned much was almost irrelevant. They learned to *think*—or were supposed to. In any event, Harvard Law School was a much tougher place than before; and the same was true of its clones. The schools had the function of filtering out the weaklings. This was a valuable help to Wall Street firms and other business lawyers, who wanted to hire the best and nothing but the best.

Compared to medical schools, law schools are cheap to run; they multiplied in the twentieth century. There were part-time schools, night schools, private and prestigious schools like Harvard and Yale, and state schools in almost every state. (By 2000, Alaska was the only state with no law school.) The elite schools supplied the great gray armies of Wall Street and its equivalents in other cities. The night schools and local schools turned out neighborhood lawyers, storefront lawyers, lawyers who handled divorces and car wrecks—and also local power elites, judges, aldermen, city councillors, and ethnic leaders.

For most of the history of the United States, lawyers were mainly "solos"; they practiced by themselves. Some lawyers banded together in partnerships; but these were typically quite small in the nineteenth century. As recently as 1950, a firm of 150 was considered a true giant. There were only a few of these firms, mostly in New York City, Chicago, and a few other metropolitan centers. But now the American army of lawyers tends more and more to be organized in law firms of breathtaking size. Today, there are firms with more than a thousand lawyers; and even in relatively small places there are firms that would have been big for New York City a short time ago. According to the lawyers directory for 2001, a firm in Providence, Rhode Island, had fifty-three lawyers; and Gough, Shanahan, Johnson & Waterman, located at 33 South Last Chance Gulch in Helena, Montana, had no fewer than eighteen. The biggest big-city firms, moreover, had begun branching out. In the 1950s, very few firms had branches: a Denver firm was a Denver firm, a Chicago firm a Chicago firm, and that was that. A few New York offices had an affiliate or two overseas; or in Washington, D.C. At the beginning of the twenty-first century, however, Baker & McKenzie, one of the biggest of law firms, had branches or affiliates in more than fifty cities, many of them overseas; Sullivan & Cromwell, a New York firm, had branches in D.C., and also in London, Paris, Melbourne, and Frankfurt, among other cities.

American lawyers do all sorts of work: they defend and prosecute criminals, they help people get divorces, sell their homes, face a tax audit, or collect on a claim from an insurance company; they sue doctors for malpractice, or defend them; they help people with wills, trusts, and the planning of estates. But overwhelmingly lawyers manage business affairs. Small firms work for small businesses, large firms work for large businesses. Some firms also handle enormous "deals," mergers of billion-dollar corporations, and mega-transactions in which one colossus swallows up another one. A giant economy—an economy measured in trillions, not billions—is an economy that generates deals, mergers, incorporations, buyouts; it is an economy with huge antitrust suits, huge tort actions, class action cases that last for years and call for whole armies of attorneys, patent and copyright matters on which the fates of industries rest, and so on endlessly. It is an economy that floats on a sea of lawyers.

All big modern economies need lawyers; the United States is not unique in this regard. It was a pioneer; but other countries seem to be catching up. The number of lawyers is growing rapidly almost everywhere: in Germany, France, and Great Britain, in Italy and Argentina and Venezuela. The exceptions are small, poor countries; and, rather oddly, some of the economic dragons of the far east. Japan, Taiwan, and Korea have very few lawyers, compared to the Western countries. They rigidly control the supply of lawyers. The bar exams are enormous hurdles: only about 2 percent of the applicants in Japan actually pass. But even Japan is under pressure to increase the size of the bar—and in Japan there are, after all, tens of thousands of law-trained people who failed the bar and cannot practice in court, but have a certain amount of legal knowledge they can use on the job. Modern economies simply cannot do without contracts, formalism, deals; modern economies cannot rely on trust and on handshakes (at least not exclusively); they must have men and women skilled at framing transactions, and at enforcing their terms. They also must have men and women who are good at running the administrative state. Government at all levels employs thousands of lawyers. And tens of thousands more in government and industry work under, with, through, or on account of law.

The demography of the American profession has undergone dramatic changes. All lawyers, until the 1870s, were men. In the last third of the century, a few bold and unusual women cracked the male monopoly. But women had only a tiny share of the population of lawyers as late as the 1950s: in 1955, women lawyers made up a little more than 1 percent of the total. Harvard opened its doors to women in 1950. In the 1960s, a flood of women hit the law schools. Women were 4 percent of the students in 1965, 16 percent in 1973, and 42 percent in 1995.[5] Women began to appear on courts as judges; in 1981, Sandra Day O'Connor became the first woman on the United States Supreme Court; Ruth Bader Ginsburg was the second. Women have served as chief justices on quite a number of state courts, including California's. And the number of black, Hispanic, and Asian lawyers and judges has also increased substantially since the 1960s.

CENTER AND PERIPHERY

The shift toward the center, toward Washington, was one of the strongest trends of the twentieth century; and continues to be strong. The federal government is one of the great growth stories of the century. How could it be otherwise? Culturally and economically, this is more and more a single country. This may seem an odd statement, in the days of plural equality. Certainly, it at least *seems* as if the country is more fragmented than ever. All over the landscape, there are vigorous identity groups, loudly claiming their rights. One can even ask (and many people do) whether there is even such a thing as America anymore; or are there simply dozens of Americas, a black America, a gay America, an Irish America, a Jewish America, an Armenian America, an America of women, old people, students, yuppies, Mormons, deaf people, and so on. Yet, ironically, one senses a growing *unity* behind the yammer of all these voices. People who are looking for their "roots" are, overwhelmingly, people who have lost those very roots; people who have become part of the great American melting pot.

All this assimilation is no accident. That there is a single economy, tightly bound together, is a reality. Goods flow easily across the borders of the states. The economy is getting more and more homogeneous. The weather in Alaska and the weather in Florida may be entirely different, but the same chain stores fill the malls, whether we are in Anchorage or Tampa. Tastes and culture are nationwide. There are, of course, regional variations; but they are getting smaller and smaller. There are differences between raunchy California and the Bible Belt, to be sure; between ice-cold Alaska and tropical Hawaii; but everybody (more or less) watches the same TV shows and movies, dances to the same noisy music, wears the same styles of clothes, sings the same songs, shops at malls that are, more and more, cookie-cutter images of one another.

According to Tip O'Neill, once speaker of the House of Representatives, all politics is local. But was Tip O'Neill really right? In a way, all politics seems to be national. The typical American sees the president on TV every day— the president, and his wife, and his family, and his associates, the house he lives in, his pets, his habits, the skeletons in his closet. The typical American could not name his state representative to save his soul, or his member of the county board. Local politics is squeezed into obscure channels and late-night programming. And, as the culture gravitates to one central point, so, too, does the law. For a good deal of our history, the states (and much of the population) resisted any form of centralization; and "states' rights" was a rallying cry. This was true not only in the south. The federal government was feeble; a Gulliver tied down with multiple ropes. All this has fundamentally changed. Basically, the federal government can do almost anything—can regulate anything—and the restrictions of federalism do not really hem it in. The habit of looking to Washington is too firmly ingrained. People demand national solutions to national problems. The Supreme Court can fine-tune the boundaries; some tasks can be handed back to the states to manage; but the core, the federal core, is almost certain to stay strong and intact. In times of crisis—the Great Depression, the two world wars, the savage attack on the World Trade Center in September 2001—the country looks to its leader, to its center, to the national government. Neither Social Security nor the atom bomb nor the war on terrorists will be handed over to Kentucky or Vermont.

This did not happen overnight, or without resistance. The New Deal was a watershed. Congress has power, under the Constitution, to regulate "interstate commerce." This was a vital power, but for much of the nineteenth century, it was hardly exercised. In the twentieth century, at least after the first years of the New Deal, it became a power to do almost *anything*. A crucial case was *Wickard v. Filburn* (1942).[6] At issue was a New Deal law, the Agricultural Adjustment Act. This law, a response to disastrously low prices for farm products, was designed to control production, and get rid of the glut on the market. Roscoe Filburn was an Ohio farmer. He sold milk, chickens, and eggs from his farm; he also planted some wheat, to feed his family and his animals. He did not sell a single grain on the market. But he grew more wheat on his farm than the AAA allowed. What could be more local, less "interstate" than Filburn's wheat, all of which went into the mouths of his family, his chickens, and his cows? But the Supreme Court upheld the law, the quota, and the fine on Filburn for over-producing. The country had thousands of Filburns, and their wheat, in the aggregate, did affect the interstate market.

Clearly, if Congress could control Filburn's wheat, it could control almost anything. In 1964, the great Civil Rights Act forbade discrimination in hotels, restaurants, and other places of public accommodation. In *Katzenbach v. McClung* (1964),[7] a unanimous Court upheld the law, and applied it to Ollie's Barbecue, a small greasy-spoon restaurant that bought all its food locally, and catered to a strictly local clientele. But some of the food it bought came from out of state; and that was enough for the Court. Cases of this sort seemed to mean that the "interstate commerce" clause was hardly any sort of re-striction on the power of Congress. Congress could, essen-tially, regulate strictly as it pleased.

Conservatives generally think all government is probably bad, and central governments the worst of all. The Supreme Court under Rehnquist showed some interest, in the last decade of the twentieth century, in breathing life into the corpse of the dead doctrine of states' rights. In one case, which startled the legal academy, the Supreme Court struck down a law on the grounds that Congress had no power to legislate on the subject. The issue was the Gun-Free School Zones Act of 1990. This law made it a federal crime to bring a gun into a school zone. Alfonso Lopez, Jr., a senior in San Antonio, carried a handgun and five bullets to school; he was caught, indicted, convicted, and sentenced to six months in jail. A bare majority of the Supreme Court reversed his conviction. Congress had full power to regulate interstate commerce; but the connection between guns, schools, and interstate commerce was simply too thin for the act to be sustained.[8]

This was the first time since New Deal days that the Court had restricted the interstate commerce power of Congress. This and other cases decided by the Rehnquist Court alarmed some legal scholars; but the cases do not go very far, and they are essentially pinpricks rather than stabs in the heart. Classic federalism is, in truth, quite dead. The federal government, especially when conservatives are in power, talks a good game about a "new" federalism, about turning power back to the states. The federal government gives out block grants to the states—big chunks of money, for welfare, or the environment, or the like—which the states can more or less spend according to their wishes and policies. But Congress can choose *not* to use block grants; or to oversee them, or not oversee them; and the huge, vast body of federal regulation still stands—the thousands of pages of the Code of Federal Regulations, which we mentioned above, have shown no signs of abating.

This does not mean, of course, that Washington runs every-thing. Besides the block grants, some strictly federal programs are, in fact, radically decentralized. "Federal" does not neces-sarily mean tightly controlled from the center; it simply means that power *could* be exercised from the center if Con-gress so decided. It sometimes does; but not always. Local of-fices, regional headquarters, and so on, shoulder an awful lot of the burden of federal regulation.

And, when all is said and done, the states remain extremely important, and powerful, as legal units. Government has ex-panded so radically in the twentieth century that the power and reach of state governments (and local governments) has *increased* radically, even as the power of these governments shrank *relatively* (relative, that is, to the federal government). They have a great deal to say about how the country is gov-erned. If you want a divorce, if you want to adopt a child, if you need to probate your aunt's estate, if you want to sue your neighbor for encroaching on your property, you do all this in a state court. Education is basically a state program. Most tort cases, most contract cases, are state cases. States control land use and many areas of health and safety. Ordinary crimes are state matters, too: it is the state, not the federal government, that tries burglars, rapists, murderers—or gives you a ticket for speeding. State prisons hold tight the vast majority of the country's prisoners. States and cities make and enforce the zoning ordinances. Building codes are local. Except for the great interstate highways, the roads that crisscross your state are state or county roads; and the streets in your city or town are local streets. The federal government has a role (and some money to spend) in all these fields; but nonetheless the fields remain largely in the province of the states. "States' rights" is still a cause and a rallying cry for conservatives. At one time, in the southern states, this was a code phrase for white supremacy—an excuse to tell the national government,

"Hands off race relations, and no interference with the 'southern way of life.'" By the end of the century, this was no longer the case. To be sure, the conservative administrations of Reagan and the two Bushes were eager to return some powers and functions to the states; even the Clinton administration did its part, allowing the states to "reform" welfare pretty much as they pleased.

But the center of *attention* has shifted, rather radically, to the center, particularly because of the mass media. Most notably, the spotlight is on the president and the presidency. The president wields extraordinary power. This is one of the most important legal stories of the twentieth century; and one of the most important stories in society at large. The "imperial presidency" is a fact of life. The president is the man with the finger on the button. He can be a small man, a limited man, even a stupid man; but the office itself can no longer be small. In foreign affairs, he holds the strings that could unleash the dogs of war. Congress has sole power to declare war, according to the Constitution. But these are now empty words. For fifty years, in effect, it is the president who declares war—declares it, runs it, ends it. And Congress rather meekly goes along. The Korean War, the war in Vietnam, the Gulf War: these were real wars, with real casualties; but in no case did Congress make the first, or decisive, move; and in most cases, Congress made no move at all.

Since at least the days of Franklin D. Roosevelt, the power of the presidency in domestic affairs has also grown enormously. The president issues "executive orders" (under the law, to be sure) that affect the lives of millions. He can turn forests into protected wilderness; or turn them into strip mines. He can declare disaster areas. He can issue rules and regulations on a wide variety of subjects. And much of this power is literally centralized within the White House. The cabinet is no longer as important as it was. True, cabinet officers are men and women of authority and substance. But they share their authority with White House staff. Domestic advisers are probably much more important in making policy than the secretaries of housing or transportation; economic advisers rival the secretary of the treasury; the national security adviser sometimes dwarfs the role of the secretary of state.

The president is also a celebrity—perhaps *the* national celebrity. His face is everywhere. Not a day goes by without his image flashing on the screen. Everybody knows what the president looks like, sounds like, walks like: what he eats, what he reads, what his family is like. They know the sound of his voice. They know or think they know something about his sex life. Much of what they think may be propaganda or fakery; but they at least have the illusion that they are peeking through the windows of the White House. And continuous exposure on television breeds a sense of familiarity.

In general, government is now visible in ways that were never true before. But what we see is of course not "government," but images and personalities. The public knows less and thinks it knows more. The upshot is what one might call the public opinion state. Because images and information (or pseudo-information) flow so quickly, because there are so many press conferences, photo opportunities, and staged events, the distance between the palaces of government and the haunts of the average Joe and Jane seems to have shrunk to almost nothing. Government and policy have an immediacy they never had before. Yet government, at all levels, is a captive of polls, focus groups, and letter-writing campaigns. It is buffeted constantly by waves of public indignation—real indignation, or fomented and manufactured indignation. In response, government at all levels fights with tricks of its own; it manipulates images; it hires and uses spin doctors; its spokesmen explain, cajole, defend, argue, twist, obfuscate, and arrange. There is a paradox: the president's power has grown enormously, including the power to control the levers of the image-makers. But he has lost some of his privacy—lost some of his ability to get away with things. Franklin D. Roosevelt was able to hide his wheelchair from the public. John F. Kennedy was able to hide his womanizing. But Richard Nixon's plots and schemes all came to light during the Watergate crisis; and William Jefferson Clinton learned he could conceal nothing—even oral sex in the Oval Office, it seems, in that most private of sanctums, came to light to embarrass the president.

Since law is the product of "government," in the broadest sense, it is deeply influenced by the facts of life in the modern state—the celebrity state, the media state, the public relations state. Laws get made and remade in a fierce storm of scandal, incident, and creative reportage. Candidates hawk programs and proposals like bars of soap or new refrigerators. Issues and policies get decided, in an important sense, in the theater of public opinion. But to create this public opinion takes money, advertising, promotion: and the policies get reduced to slogans, half-truths, sound bites.

Perhaps the cardinal fact of American life at the beginning of the twenty-first century is the sheer wealth of the country. The wealth is very unevenly distributed; but still, there is a vast middle class, certainly the majority of the population. It is a middle class that has some extra money (it works hard for it, to be sure), and some leisure—Sundays, holidays, evenings, vacations. It is a middle class that owns cars and television sets and all sorts of gadgets; and is constantly in the market for more. Above all, this is a consumer society, a society in which entertainment—fun—the filling up of those empty hours, the evenings, the weekends, the vacations—is of paramount importance.

It is also a profoundly *individualistic* society. This follows from leisure, wealth, and consumption. Individualism—

emphasis on the self, on self-realization, on personal tastes and desires—may be an inevitable aspect of capitalism. Society is saturated with advertising, and advertising is aimed at individuals: you buy as an individual, as a unique human being, with unique tastes, wants, desires (some of them manufactured). Of course, there is also family buying; but again for the unique tastes, wants, and desires of this particular family. The profound individualism of American life generates the profound individualism of American law, its emphasis on individual rights. Hence also the decline of a sense of class or class consciousness. As one author put it, social status and birth have become "no longer relevant in this ultimate democracy of spending."[9]

It seems undeniable that there is a streak of fierce individualism in American society. And rights consciousness. It is a society with many people in it who refuse to "take things lying down"; people who sue when they think their rights have been invaded. How many people? Perhaps not many. But how many are needed? How many burglars do you need, in a city, to create a crime problem? The question is not whether most people are sticklers for their rights, and sue at the drop of a hat, but whether there are more of such people than before, or more than in Finland or Japan.

An emphasis on rights. But, one may ask, aren't these rights, especially the new rights, the rights generated in the age of plural equality, rights that belong, in large degree, to *groups* rather than to individuals? Isn't this what plural equality means—group rights? Isn't this the meaning of the rise to power and influence of all the identity groups that are so salient a feature of American political, social—and legal—life: blacks and gays and the handicapped and feminists and Native Americans and so on and so forth? Yes and no; but mostly no. Group rights turn out to be, in the end, primarily individual rights. The rights of the handicapped are the rights to "mainstreaming," that is, the right to enjoy the same range of choices as everybody else. It is the right to ride the bus and the right to work on the third floor of an office building and the right to read a newspaper. If this takes a ramp or an elevator, or braille, so be it. Women's rights mean the right of women to fly a jet, dig coal, or darn socks—to have the same choices as the men do; the right, in other words, to choose these things for themselves, *as individuals*. Gay rights, student rights, the rights of Asians or Hispanics or blacks: they can all be analyzed in similar ways. The group seeks power, the group seeks rights—but why? Chiefly to allow its members to exercise the full range of individual choice, to achieve their own "personal best."

The courts are among the institutions whose job it is to enforce these rights. In the first instance, of course, the job belongs to the rest of the government: to the police, to the agencies and boards and their workers. But behind them is the power of the courts to push them into obedience. Indeed, the massive power of courts is a fact of life in the United States. This is especially true of the United States Supreme Court. It has always been an important institution—always politically significant. The infamous *Dred Scott*[10] case helped, at least in a minor way, to bring on the Civil War. Some scholars think the intransigence of state and federal courts, in the late nineteenth century and early twentieth century, had a decisive impact on the way the American labor movement developed.[11] The Supreme Court decisively intervened in the disputed presidential election of 2000, in the famous (or infamous) case of *Bush v. Gore*. Its decision—a very controversial one—in effect chose the next president of the United States (George W. Bush). In part, the Supreme Court, in this case, was overruling or forestalling actions of the Florida Supreme Court. After all, the state courts are, in their own sphere, political actors too, and often very significant ones.

Every area of law lies nakedly exposed to public opinion; but some much more than others. Criminal law—criminal justice in general—is unusually vulnerable to volcanic bursts of opinion. The media are drenched with crime stories. Crime seems almost as fascinating as sex. TV and the movies would shrivel and die without police, trials, judges, lawyers, and prisons. There is a direct connection between all this attention, and the avalanche of harsh laws, and the fact that a whole nation of people is crammed into prisons at the beginning of the twenty-first century. A child is kidnapped, raped, murdered—and the angry grief of millions turns into some draconian new law, which responds psychologically (if not logically) to the public's demands. This was the case, for example, with "Megan's Law," named after a seven-year-old girl, Megan Kanka.[12] A convicted sex offender, released from prison, and living nearby, murdered this little girl. "Megan's Law" (the original statute was passed in New Jersey) insists that sex offenders register, and be made known to neighbors, if necessary. It is a kind of leper's bell around the neck of men once convicted of sex crimes. In short order, almost every state adopted some version of "Megan's Law."

Criminal law is an extreme case; but tax law, welfare law, family law are also potentially matters that arouse the public. A major air crash, or a dramatic case of pollution, will call for equally dramatic action. Scare tactics and propaganda can also be used to *defeat* or prevent new laws, or sully the reputation of old ones. A barrage of advertisements sealed the doom of President Clinton's health plan. Insurance companies and other businesses have waged a campaign against what they consider excessive tort liability; the media eagerly join them, by publicizing horror stories, some of them totally fabricated: the psychic who got a million dollars for losing her psychic power; the old woman who got millions for spilling hot coffee on herself at McDonald's; the burglar who was hurt while he was burglarizing somebody's house, and sued the owners.[13] These probably had an impact on a public willing, apparently, to believe in the greed of their fellow citizens, and the folly of judges and juries.

And legislatures did cut back—a bit. They "capped" punitive damages, or pain and suffering, in a number of states. Still, the law explosion marches on. In 2001, one of the major issues debated in Congress was the right of patients to sue their HMOs. The administration and many Republicans resist the idea, but it may be a lost cause. There is too much demand for action, too many tales of misconduct floating about, too many people who consider themselves victims of insurance companies and HMOs. At this writing, the betting is that this new cause of action will eventually be born.

The dominance of public opinion, scandal, incident, in the formation of law, is mute testimony to the rampant power of the media—and especially television. Television, among other things, presents us with the illusion of an all-seeing eye. It allows us to enter worlds that were at one time totally closed to us—private worlds. Television created the celebrity society. It fills our lives with gossip and images of the rich and powerful, politicians, religious leaders, rock stars, baseball players, movie stars. It creates the illusion that these celebrities are part of our lives, so that when Princess Diana died, thousands of people were grief-stricken, as if they had known her. In a sense they had. Or thought so.

Television molds and reshapes the very meaning of authority. Political leaders become celebrities. Image is everything. George Washington had wooden teeth; was he a wooden speaker, too? Did he have "charisma"? Did Jefferson? It hardly mattered. Today it is essential. Even such religious leaders as the pope and the dalai lama have become celebrities, familiar faces, familiar voices. Prior popes and lamas were austere, distant figures, immured in their palaces. But the celebrity nature of authority, of leadership, means that society is governed, not so much by the invisible hand, as by the visible tube. The president, as we noted, has become a celebrity; he is, in fact, as Neal Gabler puts it, the "entertainer-in-chief." After all, if image is everything, then a president is judged by his image, and the line between politics and entertainment blurs, if it does not downright disappear. Politics—again, as Neal Gabler puts it—is just "show business for ugly people."[14]

Television also alters the meaning of "privacy." It breaks down barriers between reality and entertainment. Thousands of people seem to lust after their fifteen minutes of fame. Millions watch the "trash talk shows," or *Big Brother*, or *Survivor*, and some portion of these millions are also willing to be *part* of one of these shows. The "reality" programs are "reality" only in a limited sense—but the participants are not actors (at any rate, not supposed to be); and they use their own names, and express their own personalities. The Internet, too, makes it possible for everyone to be a star.

We live in a Peeping Tom society, and this has vast implications. Politics has become just another reality show, like *Survivor* or *Big Brother*. The electorate is the audience. The campaign is the show. On election day, the audience chooses which competing player goes to Washington, which one goes home in disgrace. Since these "shows" require vast amounts of money for advertising, brochures, mass meetings, mailings, and above all money to buy television time (which is enormously expensive), politics more than ever depends on the mad scramble for cash. Running for office means a constant wheedling for money. All money has strings attached. That this has an impact on the structure of politics, and on the structure of *policy*, is too obvious for words. The shape of legislation is impacted—beyond a doubt. Exactly how much is not so easy to tell.

Nobody can predict the future. The "law explosion" might, just possibly, reach some sort of plateau. That it would go backward seems almost inconceivable. Society is too thoroughly legalized. Too many aspects of law are part of the culture; the roots of legalization lie too deep in the bowels of the social order. An individualistic, consuming, wealthy society; a free market, free trade society; a society of plural equality—such a society cannot do without an enormous umbrella of law and legal process. Law is the glue that binds the cells of Leviathan's body; and the body of society itself.

NOTES

1. 9 CFR sec. 93.105.

2. 21 CFR secs. 173.5, 173.10.

3. 29 CFR sec. 1606.7

4. The standard history of legal education is Robert B. Stevens, *Law School: Legal Education in America from the 1850s to the 1980s* (1983).

5. Lawrence M. Friedman, *American Law in the Twentieth Century* (2002), p. 458.

6. 317 U.S. 111 (1942).

7. 379 U.S. 294 (1964).

8. The case was *United States v. Lopez,* 514 U.S. 549 (1995).

9. Gary Cross, *An All-Consuming Century: Why Commercialism Won in Modern America* (2000), pp. 21–22.

10. *Dred Scott v. Sandford,* 19 How. (60 U.S.) 393 (1857); see Don E. Fehrenbacher, *The Dred Scott Case: Its Significance in American Law and Politics* (1976).

11. See William E. Forbath, *Law and the Shaping of the American Labor Movement* (1991).

12. Megan's Law is New Jersey Stats. Ann. 2C:7-1 through 7-11 (1994).

13. See Robert M. Hayden, "The Cultural Logic of a Political Crisis:

Common Sense, Hegemony and the Great American Liability Insurance Famine of 1986," *Studies in Law, Politics, and Society*, Vol. 11 (1991), p. 95.

14. Neal Gabler, *Life the Movie: How Entertainment Conquered Reality* (1998), p. 117.

NOTES FOR FURTHER READING

There is a huge literature on the American legal tradition, and it seems to be growing all the time. Much of the literature is relatively recent. But even though the material is piling up, and a lot of it is of high quality, there are still very few *general* accounts—books that try to survey the whole landscape of American law, historically speaking. One of this small band is Kermit Hall's book *The Magic Mirror: Law in American History* (1989). My own work *A History of American Law* (2d ed., 1985) is less comprehensive than the title seems to suggest; in fact, my treatment of the twentieth century is quite skimpy. I have tried to fill this gap in a recent book, *American Law in the Twentieth Century* (2002). The general treatment of constitutional history that I find most compelling is Melvin I. Urofsky and Paul Finkelman's *A March of Liberty: A Constitutional History of the United States* (two volumes, 2d ed., 2001)—this work is, in fact, much broader than a constitutional history. Histories of the law in individual states are also extremely rare; one exception is Joseph A. Ranney's *Trusting Nothing to Providence: A History of Wisconsin's Legal System* (1999).

A lot has been written about the law of the colonial period. One of the foundational works is George L. Haskins's *Law and*

Authority in Early Massachusetts: A Study in Tradition and Design (1960); other notable works on colonial times include David T. Konig's *Law and Society in Puritan Massachusetts: Essex County, 1629–1692* (1979), Bruce H. Mann's *Neighbors and Strangers: Law and Community in Early Connecticut* (1987), and Peter C. Hoffer's *Law and People in Colonial America* (1992). Marylynn Salmon's *Women and the Law of Property in Early America* (1986) takes up a much neglected subject. On the transition to the republican period, see William E. Nelson's *Americanization of the Common Law: The Impact of Legal Change on Massachusetts Society, 1760–1830* (1975).

There are many treatments of the nineteenth and twentieth century, but they tend to confine themselves to particular subjects or fields of law, and this bibliographical essay will do the same. To begin with, there is a considerable literature on criminal law and criminal justice. Here I can cite my own book *Crime and Punishment in American History* (1993), a general account of the subject. Two studies of the nineteenth century are particularly worth reading: Michael Hindus's *Prison and Plantation: Crime, Justice, and Authority in Massachusetts and South Carolina, 1767–1878* (1980) and Edward L. Ayers's *Vengeance and Justice: Crime and Punishment in the 19th Century American South* (1984); see also Lawrence M. Friedman and Robert V. Percival's *The Roots of Justice: Crime and Punishment in Alameda County, California, 1870–1910* (1981). Homicide has had its chroniclers: see Roger Lane's *Violent Death in the City: Suicide, Accident, and Murder in Nineteenth-Century Philadelphia* (1979) and *Murder in America: A History* (1997), as well as Eric Monkkonen's *Murder in New York City* (2001); on the regulation of sexuality, see Mary E. Odem's *Delinquent Daughters: Protecting and Policing Adolescent Female Sexuality in the United States, 1885–1920* (1995) and David J. Langum's *Crossing Over the Line: Legislating Morality and the Mann Act* (1994); on the police, there is Eric Monkkonen's book *Police in Urban*

America, 1860–1920 (1981), David R. Johnson's *American Law Enforcement: A History* (1981), and Robert M. Fogelson's *Big-City Police* (1977); on prisons (and other institutions), there is David Rothman's compelling though controversial book *The Discovery of the Asylum: Social Order and Disorder in the New Republic* (1971); more recently, there is Adam J. Hirsch's *The Rise of the Penitentiary: Prisons and Punishment in Early America* (1992). James B. Jacobs's *Stateville: The Penitentiary in Mass Society* (1977) is a good study of a particular prison. On capital punishment, the best account is Stuart Banner's very recent book, *The Death Penalty: An American History* (2002).

On family law and related matters, there are now the beginnings of a respectable literature. I want to mention the following: Michael Grossberg's *Governing the Hearth: Law and the Family in Nineteenth-Century America* (1985), Hendrik Hartog's *Man and Wife in America: A History* (2000), and Nancy Cott's *Public Vows: A History of Marriage and the Nation* (2000). Herbert Jacob's *Silent Revolution: The Transformation of Divorce Law in the United States* (1988) deals with the rise of no-fault divorce. Carole Shammas, Marylynn Salmon, and Michel Dahlin, in *Inheritance in America: From Colonial Times to the Present* (1987), have shed light on an obscure but important aspect of the law, one that is relevant both to family life and to the economy.

There is a huge body of work on slavery, and since slavery was a legal status (among other things), general works on slavery necessarily touch on the law of slavery, including the classic study by Kenneth Stampp, *The Peculiar Institution: Slavery in the Ante-Bellum South* (1956). There are many monographs on slavery in various states and regions; one good, recent example is Larry Eugene Rivers's *Slavery in Florida: Territorial Days to Emancipation* (2000). Specifically on the legal aspects of slavery, see Thomas D. Morris's *Southern Slavery and the Law, 1619–1860* (1996), Ariela Gross's *Double Character: Slavery and Mastery in the Antebellum Southern Courtroom* (2000), and Don Fehrenbacher's *The Dred Scott Case: Its Significance in American Law and Politics* (1978); an abridged edition of Fehrenbacher's weighty book was published in 1981, under the title *Slavery, Law, and Politics: The Dred Scott Case in Historical Perspective;* on slavery and the criminal law, see Philip J. Schwarz's *Twice Condemned: Slaves and the Criminal Laws of Virginia, 1705–1865* (1988). After emancipation came Reconstruction, then the long night of white supremacy. A brilliant and disturbing portrait of this period is Leon Litwack's *Trouble in Mind: Black Southerners in the Age of Jim Crow* (1998).

Government regulation and economic matters have drawn their share of attention. William J. Novak's *The People's Welfare: Law and Regulation in Nineteenth-Century America* (1996) is a richly detailed account of what government actually did in a period often written off as laissez-faire. Also important are two books by Morton Keller, *Regulating a New Economy: Public Policy and Economic Change in America, 1900–1933* (1990) and *Regulating a New Society: Public Policy and Social Change in America, 1900–1933* (1994); see also Herbert Hovenkamp's *Enterprise and American Law, 1836–1937* (1991). There are significant studies of particular fields of economic law, beginning perhaps with J. Willard Hurst's classic and massive study, *Law and Economic Growth: The Legal History of the Lumber Industry in Wisconsin, 1836–1915* (1964); see also Tony A. Freyer's *Forums of Order: The Federal Courts and Business in American History* (1979), Robert S. Hunt's *Law and Locomotives: The Impact of the Railroad on Wisconsin Law in the Nineteenth Century* (1958), Harry N. Scheiber's *Ohio Canal Era: A Case Study of Government and the Economy, 1820–1861* (1969), William Letwin's *Law and Economic Policy in America: The Evolution of the Sherman Antitrust Act* (1965), and James W. Ely, Jr.'s *Railroads and American Law* (2002). On labor and labor regulation, see Christopher L. Tomlins's *Law, Labor, and Ideology in the Early American Republic* (1993), William Forbath's *Law and the Shaping of the American*

Labor Movement (1991), and Melvyn Dubofsky's *The State and Labor in Modern America* (1994).

The literature on civil rights and civil liberties is staggering in bulk. There are dozens of books and articles on *Brown v. Board of Education,* what came before it, and what came after. A fascinating account of the case and its history can be found in Richard Kluger's *Simple Justice: The History of Brown v. Board of Education and Black America's Struggle for Equality* (1976); a recent treatment is James T. Patterson's *Brown v. Board of Education: A Civil Rights Milestone and Its Troubled Legacy* (2001); see also Michal Belknap's *Federal Law and Southern Order: Racial Violence and Constitutional Conflict in the Post-Brown South* (1995) and Mary L. Dudziak's *Cold War Civil Rights: Race and the Image of American Democracy* (2000). An interesting aspect of the development of modern civil rights doctrine is covered in Shawn Francis Peters's book, *Judging Jehovah's Witnesses: Religious Persecution and the Dawn of the Rights Revolution* (2000). On the work of the Warren court, which played such a significant role in the development of modern rights law, see Morton Horwitz's *The Warren Court and the Pursuit of Justice* (1998) and Lucas A. Powe, Jr.'s *The Warren Court and American Politics* (2000). There is a growing literature, too, on *Roe v. Wade,* very notably David J. Garrow's *Liberty and Sexuality: The Right to Privacy and the Making of Roe v. Wade* (1994); a shorter and very readable treatment of the case, its background, and its consequences is N.E.H. Hull and Peter Charles Hoffer's *Roe v. Wade: The Abortion Rights Controversy in American History* (2001). The Hull and Hoffer book is one of a series of short books, published by the University Press of Kansas and edited by Hoffer and Hull, under the general title Landmark Law Cases and American Society; another example is William E. Nelson's *Marbury v. Madison: The Origins and Legacy of Judicial Review* (2000).

Roe v. Wade, Brown v. Board of Education, Marbury v. Madison, and the *Dred Scott* case are not the only decisions to have whole books to themselves. In fact, when a book of this kind is good, it does not confine itself to the case, but discusses the context, the soil out of which the case grew, and how it affected society. Among the books that do this, for a case or a group of cases, are Stanley I. Kutler's *Privilege and Creative Destruction: The Charles River Bridge Case* (1971), Richard Polenberg's *Fighting Faiths: The Abrams Case, the Supreme Court, and Free Speech* (1987), and Arthur Sabin's *Red Scare in Court: New York Versus the International Workers Order* (1993).

There is no general history of the legal profession, but the material on the role of the profession in J. Willard Hurst's *The Growth of American Law: The Law Makers* (1950) is still of great value; a good deal of history, too, is found in Richard L. Abel's book *American Lawyers* (1989); another standard work is Jerold S. Auerbach's *Unequal Justice: Lawyers and Social Change in Modern America* (1976); on the earlier profession, see Gerard W. Gawalt's *The Promise of Power: The Emergence of the Legal Profession in Massachusetts, 1760–1840* (1979). There is some work on particular branches of the profession; see, for example, William G. Thomas's *Lawyering for the Railroad: Business, Law, and Power in the New South* (1999) and Peter H. Irons's *The New Deal Lawyers* (1982). Biographies (and autobiographies) of lawyers are plentiful, but few of them are any good. I have liked, in particular, Kevin Tierney's *Darrow: A Biography* (1979), William Harbaugh's *Lawyer's Lawyer: The Life of John W. Davis* (1973), and David J. Langum's *William M. Kunstler: The Most Hated Lawyer in America* (1999). On legal education see Robert B. Stevens's *Law School: Legal Education in America from the 1850s to the 1980s* (1983); see also William P. LaPiana's *Logic and Experience: The Origin of Modern American Legal Education* (1994).

Judges and their work are the subject of a massive literature. Probably every Supreme Court justice has a biographer of sorts, and the famous ones, like Oliver Wendell Holmes, Jr., and Earl Warren, have whole bookshelves all to themselves. Again, many of the biographies are too respectful, and most of them are not very good, but a few are outstanding. I recommend in particular Charles Fairman's *Mr. Justice Miller and the Supreme Court, 1862–1890* (1939); G. Edward White's *Justice Oliver Wendell Holmes: Law and the Inner Self* (1993) and White's book on Earl Warren, *Earl Warren: A Public Life* (1982); Richard Polenberg's *The World of Benjamin Cardozo: Personal Values and the Judicial Process* (1997); and Laura Kalman's *Abe Fortas: A Biography* (1990). There is an ongoing project (it has been ongoing for decades) to compile a huge, multivolume history of the United States Supreme Court. The general title is *History of the Supreme Court of the United States.* Many (but not all) of the volumes have appeared. Each has its own author. Each is, shall we say, of formidable length; they are valuable as reference books, but the general reader is not likely to have the time or the patience to plow through these volumes. Kermit L. Hall has edited *The Oxford Guide to United States Supreme Court Decisions* (1999), a collection of short, snappy, and on the whole well-crafted essays on the major decisions of the Court. An unusual and fascinating work is Peter Irons's book *The Courage of Their Convictions* (1988); Irons tells the story of sixteen important Supreme Court cases, not through the eyes of lawyers or judges, but through interviews with the men and women who were the major litigants.

On the nature of American legal culture, the seminal work of J. Willard Hurst, perhaps the greatest of American legal historians, is still essential reading. His study of the lumber industry and *The Growth of American Law* have already been mentioned; of his many other books, perhaps the best known, and the most accessible, is *Law and the Conditions of Freedom in the Nineteenth-Century United States* (1956). Morton J. Horwitz's book *The Transformation of American Law, 1780–1860* (1977) advanced an important and somewhat controversial thesis on the nature of American law during the period he covered. Horwitz's more recent book *The Transformation of American Law, 1870–1960: The Crisis of Legal Orthodoxy* (1992) focuses more exclusively on legal thought. I have also tried to deal with American legal culture, and its character past and present, in a series of books: *Total Justice* (1985), *The Republic of Choice: Law, Authority, and Culture* (1990), and *The Horizontal Society* (1999). A recent and incisive critique of the legal tradition is Robert A. Kagan's *Adversarial Legalism: The American Way of Law* (2001). Scholars will continue, of course, to try to plumb the mysteries of the legal system, historically and otherwise. The past, like memory itself, is in many ways an artifact of the present. Each generation sees it through its own particular lens.

INDEX

About the Author

LAWRENCE M. FRIEDMAN is Marion Rice Kirkwood Professor of Law at Stanford University. He is the author or editor of twenty-three books, including *The Legal System: A Social Science Perspective, American Law in the Twentieth Century, A History of American Law,* and *Crime and Punishment in American History.* Professor Friedman is a fellow of the American Academy of Arts and Sciences and the recipient of numerous awards.

A Note on the Type

The principal text of this Modern Library edition
was set in a digitized version of Janson, a typeface that
dates from about 1690 and was cut by Nicholas Kis,
a Hungarian working in Amsterdam. The original matrices have
survived and are held by the Stempel foundry in Germany.
Hermann Zapf redesigned some of the weights and sizes for
Stempel, basing his revisions on the original design.